DISSIDENTLY SPEAKING

CHANGE THE WORDS
CHANGE THE WAR

DISSIDENTLY SPEAKING

CHANGE THE WORDS.
CHANGE THE WAR.

BRENT E HAMACHEK

PIERUCCI PUBLISHING
ELEVATING WORLD CONSCIOUSNESS
THROUGH STORIES.

Published by Pierucci Publishing, P.O. Box 2074, Carbondale, Colorado 81623, USA
www.pieruccipublishing.com

Cover design by Felisa Blazek
Edited by Joan Matthews

Ebook ISBN: 978-1-962578-09-7
Hardcover ISBN: 978-1-962578-08-0
Paperback ISBN: 978-1-962578-11-0

Library of Congress Control Number: 2024900399

Pierucci Publishing books may be purchased in bulk at special discounts for sales promotion, corporate gifts, fund-raising, or educational purposes. Special editions can be created to specifications. For details, contact the Special Sales Department, Pierucci Publishing, PO Box 2074, Carbondale, CO 81623 or Publishing@PierucciPublishing.com or toll-free telephone at 1-855-720-1111.

For Jonah, Marlie, Shane, and Therese.
Four very courageous young people
who gave me hope from Hope in Autumn 2023.

TABLE OF CONTENTS

Acknowledgments 1

Foreword 5

Introduction: An Idea For Assessing America 230+ Years In . . .13
    Composing Dissidently Speaking 19
    A Right to Write 22
    A New American Operating Agreement 24
    Goals for This Book 26
    History Doesn't Repeat Itself 32

Chapter One: An Idea for Ending Our National Division 41
    Symptoms of a National Behavioral and Language Disorder 41
    America Is Going Out of Business 46
    The Incoherence of "Team Right" and "Team Left" 46
    More Headline Nonsense 48
    Four Wrongs Don't Make a Right 51
    The Exact Problem We Face with Right-Left Labels 53
    Origins of a Divided American Species 55
    The French Revolution: The Birth of "Right Wing" and "Left
        Wing" 56
    The Russian Revolution: Lenin Co-opts the "Left" 57
    Mussolini, Hitler, Fascism, Nazism, and Choosing Sides in
        World War II 58
    Post World War II "Hunts for Communists"—U.S. Teams
        Start to Form 60
    The Civil Rights Movement and Civil Rights Act—New
        Team Members Recruited 62
    The Corporal Turned Führer in Germany 64
    Vietnam—Team Right and Team Left Pick Up (Lay Down)
        Their Weapons 65
    Roe v. Wade Translates into Right v. Left 67
    A Series of Unfortunate Events Helps Both Teams Complete
        Their Rosters 70

Team Right and Team Left "Platoons"—The American
    Political Operating Model 74
Never Let a Division Go to Waste 82
The REAL Political Continuum 84
Pulling It All Together 87
It is the same for a nation and its people. 88
Take the "Left-Right News Challenge" 91

Chapter Two: An Idea for Healing Our Personal Divisions. . . . 95
From 30,000 feet—A Look at the Problem 96
Myth: "There are two sides to everything." 98
My Facts, Your Facts, Our Facts, No Facts 99
Perspective, Prejudice, and Noise 100
Perspective and Prejudice: Your Vantage Point with
    Obstructed Views. 101
Hearing Through the Noise: Facts Whisper, but Fancy Screams. . 106
The Perils of Paraphrasing 108
All Opinions Are Not Created Equal! 111
The Personal Economics of Opinions: Investment, Sunk
    Cost, Marginal Cost and Benefit 114
Why Issues-Based Conversations Go Bad Fast 117
So What Do We Do Now? (Or Should We Just Fight About It?). . 118

Chapter Three: An Idea for Kicking a Bad Communal Habit. 123
The Cue-Reward-Response Addiction Cycle. 124
How Friends Become Conflict-Wielding Foes. 128
Your Brain on Conflict 129
Americans in Fight-or-Flight 130
America's Confrontation Dealers. 132
Our Journey—A Look at Causes of Effects 133
Doing Better: Everything Is Personal. 142
Doing Better: "Tolerance" and "Surrender" Are Not Synonyms. . 144
Doing Better: Not About Splitting the Difference 146
Doing Better: Love Thy Neighbor 148

Chapter Four: An Idea About Dissidently Speaking. 155
We Have Traveled Far (in the Wrong Direction) 156
This Is Not About an Election 160
What Is the Societal Structure Facing a Dissident? 163
By What Right 167

Rules for Becoming an Effective Dissident 170
This Has Been Done Before............................. 181
Postscript 183

**Chapter Five: An Idea About the Thin Line Between Good
and Evil** 187
I'm ethical. Are you ethical? 190
Hobbes Was Right! 192
Duty as a Differentiator 197
What Can Be Done (. . . If Anything)?.................. 202

Addendum A Declination of Codependence 207
American Declination of Codependence 210

Index 215

ACKNOWLEDGMENTS

For a writer, I think this is the most rewarding part of a literary project, one from which I have been denied enjoyment up to this point, owing to the fact that I've been either writing as a ghost, or writing alongside those with a much shinier nom de plume. I now have the opportunity to say my own thank-you to the people who have both made my writing possible and helped to create the ideas that form the content.

First on the list is Charlie Kirk, the founder of Turning Point USA and, in some real sense, the founder of me; at least when it comes to my having been given a voice in the world of ideas. I was a 51-year-old business consultant when I was introduced to the then 19-year-old founder of what would become in a decade's time the largest conservative campus organization in the country. Sitting at a dinner table over a lengthy evening conversation, that teenager spotted something in me that nobody had ever before glimpsed, save perhaps for myself a full 30 years previously. He gave me the chance to contribute to TPUSA by writing much of their early campus literature, a task that ultimately led to my writing his first book with him, Time for a Turning Point. I thank him before every public appearance I make. Comrade Kirk, I am in your debt.

An important P.S. to the Charlie Kirk note is a thank you to my friend Bill Frech, who insisted on making the introduction. I honestly thought the idea was a little, well, misplaced. Bill didn't. He made it happen. He is my unmoved mover.

While I just gave Charlie Kirk the credit for launching me, there was another person who gets credit for my sort of "pre-launch." That would be now Professor Emeritus, but from 1980 to 1984, my professor at Lake Superior State University, Gary Johnson. Gary was the person who taught all my political science courses and was everything a professor is meant to be. To this day, I have no idea what his positions are on absolutely any issue. What he did teach me to do was to ask questions and to think. He was relentless in forcing his students to defend their positions logically and consistently. I have tried my best in the decades since to always think through the gaps or inconsistencies in my own arguments before making them. For over 40 years I have been asking myself the question: How would Professor Johnson challenge me? Thank you, Gary, for impacting my thought processes. You were with me in every sentence of this book.

I could not have assembled this work properly or professionally without the support and comprehensive skills of my friend, Stephanie Pierucci of Pierucci Publishing. When I decided I wanted to do this, I knew there was only one person in this industry whom I could trust to give me the combination of honesty, criticism, and capability necessary to yield a product of quality that would also satisfy my own quirkish requirements. Stephanie wasn't my first choice; she was my only choice. What readers think will be up to them, but I am, without equivocation, certain I have chosen brilliantly.

In yet another excellent choice, my friend and business colleague, Cody Peters, has been instrumental in the digital "advancement" of this work. In order for an average old mind to be heard, it needs a brilliant young mind to help present and amplify. My relationship with Cody began several years ago when I acted as a bit of a business mentor. Today, the student has become the master and I learn from him on almost a daily basis. Thank you, my friend, and a big thanks to your business partner Jonathan Torres who did such brilliant work on the book website.

My friend and near-neighbor, Joan Matthews, took the mess that was my original copy and edited it masterfully. I believe she made about 1,000 corrections and offered another 1,000 suggestions (999 of which I accepted). She did not edit this paragraph (how tacky would that be?), so it is likely filled with errors. Forgive me, Joan, for any miscues in this thank-you, but accept my sincerest offering of gratitude for the work you've done. All the criticisms I receive for this book will be for what I wrote, not for commas, colons, or syntax.

For over a decade, my dear friend Tamara Leigh has been right beside me listening to my ideas develop, encouraging me to write, to speak, and to stick my head out from the shell in which, left to my own devices, I would be far too comfortable to let it remain. She has introduced me to half the people I know and about ninety percent of the ones that matter. She is the first domino to fall in so many threads in my life, and yet still she stands. She was the original person with whom I shared my Team Right–Team Left paradigm, and she was tireless in insisting that I publish the work. Charlie

Kirk might have provided the vehicle, but Tamara loaded the wagon. Thank you, Tamara, for the push (and the push . . . and the push . . . and . . .).

Finally, there is the woman whose name appears scattered within these pages but whose presence fills them, Felisa Blazek. She has had the most extraordinary impact on all my thought processes. The visionary behind the Common Ground Campus program, she has revealed to me the impossible, that being the notion that dichotomies can be reconciled. Before her, I used to think with a limp, strongly favoring my "right" side. Her ability to take fire and ice and meld them into warmth has helped me to straighten my gait and balance my thoughts. Prior to our collaborations, I may have thought about many of the things I've shared in this collection, but I would not have chosen the same words. I was of the mind that ceding any ground to an opposing view was a sign of weakness, but the strongest person I know has taught me just the opposite is true. I have learned that the surest way to make a firm, thoughtful stand is to allow your mind to be in constant motion, and that by reaching out and understanding others, you can better reach and understand yourself. She literally designed the outer cover of this book, and has metaphorically designed much of what's found within its pages. Thank you, Felisa. As you like to say in the Common Ground Campus program, you have forced me to do better.

FOREWORD

It's both my personal conviction and my professional responsibility to help others understand that words change the world. Nevertheless, my life has been a painful exercise not in learning how to use words *well*, but in learning how *not to* waste them or even wield them in a way that hurts myself and others.

What "Dissidently Speaking" teaches me, now in my third reading, is that we haven't just destroyed language with divisive political terms and labels that we use flippantly and irresponsibly in everyday conversation, but that we destroy one another.

I am guilty of fueling that division in my community and, sometimes, even in my own home. It is for that reason that I see the publishing and promoting of this book as a mission in my life, to better my world.

"A house divided against itself cannot stand," said President Abraham Lincoln. It's easy to see that by sequestering one another through language, we become a less powerful force against whatever restless and tireless evil clearly seeks to dominate us. With his masterful wordsmithing, Brent Hamachek paints a picture that levels the playing field, compelling the reader to inspect the plank in his own eye, so to speak, before trying to remove the speck in another's.

Although the contents of "Dissidently Speaking" is jam-packed with great ideas, the book is also a pleasure to read for anybody who understands that words change the world, for better or worse, and who wants to be part of the solution, not the problem. With that said, I encourage the reader to pay attention and mindfully dedicate a few weeks or so to taking patient nibbles on this content. Then allow those nibbles to digest as you objectively observe your environment. What previously haunted your days, manifesting as spooky ghosts that sabotage conversation and relationships from the most basic interactions at the post office to statements from our highest profile political pundits, will look less mysterious. This book will give you the eyes to see those boogiemen, and the tools to avoid their snares.

I suspect you can't read a single chapter of this manuscript and remain unchanged, at least in your thinking. Above all, that is Brent's sacred intention with this book: that we would be better thinkers. The unstated theme of the book, if I may, seems to be materializing in ways I didn't expect. In short, it is through the lessons and ideas in this book that I have found myself becoming more equanimous and collaborative with those around me, particularly those with whom I have perceived political differences. Simply stated, "Dissidenly Speaking" has materially helped me become a more loving person and to see the world for what it is; a complex system that deserves more than binary language and red versus blue radicalism that is designed to separate us from our power, our dollars and, even, our freedom.

"I would argue that the two-party system is the single-most responsible factor in the division of our country today. It forces complex decisions into a binary structure," states Hamachek in "Dissidently Speaking." In the following stories, you'll see how being forced into the binary structure Brent identifies above caused me to lose a dear friend, but also helped me identify the perceived divide between myself and somebody with whom I wasn't destined to be friends when the two-party binary structure is applied, but with whom I was able to circumvent such division to enjoy common ground and even genuine respect for one another.

I've had the honor of working with Brent on a number of projects over the years. In both professional collaboration and friendship, I am continually inspired by Brent's quick wit. He'd never own this and I frankly doubt he'll even allow me to sing his praises in his own book foreword.

That said, one unexpected gift from "Dissidently Speaking" is my new ability to get a glimpse at how Brent's brilliant mind works, and why he seems largely unperturbed and at peace with the world around him. Case in point: we became friends during the early stages of the plandemic and at a time when Brent soberly said one day over waffles and my tantruming toddler, "well, I guess I'll never get to go to a Bruce Springsteen concert again."

If you know Brent, you know that he has a song lyric, particularly a Springsteen one, at the ready to surmise or punctuate almost any phone call or conversation.

"How do you not feel seriously pissed about that?" I asked, genuinely surprised.

Brent stated that there was no sense in getting emotional, because the war wouldn't be won by flinging F bombs all over what we then called

"Twitter." He told me something that I later brought back home to Aspen, Colorado and spoke about almost daily with my community; a lesson about being a dissident. Brent distilled that lesson in this book.

> *Do some basic math. Assume there are 330 million people in this country. Then assume that half of them (165 million) are [either active or passive dissidents]. Finally, assume that everyone of those 165 million engage in at least one form of dissident activity. Eventually there will be that straw that breaks the totalitarian back. You could be that straw.*

I could be that straw, or I could inspire another to be that straw. But I won't get there by wielding words like an unsupervised toddler with a crayon box in front of a freshly painted white wall. I get to be that inspiring force when I think critically, engage in honest conversation, honor the perspectives of others, refuse to see everybody as either "red" or "blue," and when I say less and listen more.

Brent likens this book to throwing your linguistic toybox all over the floor. After a couple of careful, mindful readings through "Dissidently Speaking," I can say with confidence that you will never be the same, provided you allow your language patterns to get dissected and doodled on in the process.

As for my personal experiences with "Dissidently Speaking," during the winter of 2023 I had my first significant encounter with the book. Sadly, this ended in the loss of a dear friend who perceived herself to be on the opposite side of an unnecessary and redundant war she thought we needed to wage simply because I used sympathetic language for the victims of the October 7th tragedy on both sides. In my friend's world, there was only a murderer and a victim; surely there couldn't be complexity when it comes to war…

That once dear friend and I had a failure to communicate, although we were closer to the same side than we consciously perceived in that moment, and at least I felt that I was teachable on the subject. My refusal to come to a black and white decision about the complex conflict in the Middle East (that is the result of millenia of tension and countless other conflicts and wars) erupted into my friend stooping to hurtful name-calling, which resulted in words that won't be forgotten. I was being bullied to choose a side. Upon my refusal to identify with a side, I was deemed a traitor, a corporate shill, a Zionist, and even a murderer by the friend. Yeah, those are words I won't forget.

A few days later while still acutely mourning my loss I called Brent and said, "if only she had read your book, perhaps she would have thought twice before the unnecessary verbal annihilation. What hurt the most is that we're on the same team ninety-nine percent of the time."

Again in January of 2024 I had an unforgettable encounter with "Dissidently Speaking." I was not on vacation, but I was on Maui, Hawaii on actual business. I'm still pissed that there was no sunbathing, snorkeling nor surfing involved in that week on Maui, if you can't tell. The fact that I was in paradise and unable to milk it for at least a suntan in the middle of January made me a bit less patient than usual.

After a grueling couple of days of travel and being thrust into hard, emotionally taxing work from the moment I stepped off the plane, I sat down for my first meal in at least two days. A text from one of my cookbook authors came in. "Stephanie. Get on the phone immediately. We have an opportunity to do a book tour at the Sundance Film Festival at some elite parties."

I ignored the text. My Hawaiian host had set a plate of venison in front of me that he and his friends had just acquired on a hunting trip and I was famished.

Another text came into state the obvious. "Stephanie, I'm calling." And another, "please pick up the phone!"

Then he pulled out the big guns. The mother of a famous actress and dear friend texted me. "Steph, this is it. You have to be on this call."

My author, a celebrity chef and restaurateur, had been invited to cater a party for some Hollywood folks at the festival. Was he going to get the opportunity to be on a TV Show or the star of a documentary? Curiosity killed me and I regretfully answered his third call, leaving my gracious host at the table, alone.

The individuals on the phone that night presented a strong case that our involvement in the festival would provide my author with funding for a fairly revolutionary food concept. The hostess had invited several successful businessmen and women, including restaurateurs who were interested in the author's work.

In no time at all I was thrust into three weeks of a chaotic three ring circus, a tedious, tiring, and unpaid task I would have been best to avoid. If only I'd have turned my phone on silent and spent my night recuperating from travel and the true crime investigation I'd been conducting on Maui.

A few nights before the Sundance event, one of the parties close to the Park City socialite who was hosting the event called me to report that the hostess was $30,000 over budget on the event and they expected *me* to bully and badger my network for sponsors. What's more, since my author was being featured at the event, they proceeded to berate me for "mooching" off their networks, telling me that I should pay a sponsorship fee to be in the room. I bit my tongue but wanted to tell them I'd fork over a fee *not* to be in that room with all those mother-WEF'ers.

Over the next several days, individuals from New York to Seattle called me incessantly at all hours, begging me to do publicity for the event, find promotional partners, and squeeze sponsorship money from my network.

I was aghast.

I determined I'd arrive in Utah and make some heads roll and, at the last minute, I made the wise decision to stay home. Unfortunately, the sous-chef canceled after her Aunt died and I allowed my generous codependent nature to get the best of me.

I arrived in Park City on a Thursday night at 1:15 a.m. after sliding into a ditch some thirty or forty miles outside of "Dinosaur, Colorado." *Or was I in Utah?* It had been hours since I'd seen Rifle. It was frigid in late January and I was on a two-lane street that had been icy. For at least an hour ortwoIwascrawlingat15mphaveragespeed. And...I had been drinking coffee. A lot of it. I had to pull over. Sadly, I didn't pull over onto what I perceived to be a flat ramp on the side of the road. It was a steep ditch that only appeared to be flat due to the width of a snow plow, I learned quickly. I ended up trying to dig my car out of the snow without a shovel for nearly an hour before an electrician with a utility company emergency found me on the side of the road and, God bless him, pulled me out of the snow.

Now I'm not just indignant, but exhausted, too. I had every intention of showing up at this event, helping my author/chef for a day or two, and leaving on Friday night after a scheduled party ended. I didn't want to spend a moment longer with these fools than I had to. As it turns out, I hadn't left by Saturday, or even Sunday. I left Monday morning at 12:15 a.m. and drove back to Aspen in the middle of the night, staying at the event and soaking everybody and everything up right to the last drop.

What changed?

Clearly something downright extraordinary happened that weekend.

On the first night of the event I was standing in front of a sink washing a Vitamix in scalding hot water for my author and privately playing the world's smallest violin for what a terrible person I was to let these characters walk all over me and rope me into this hellish experience. I had been the kitchen wench standing in front of that sink for at least eight hours at that point, near one or two in the morning.

One of the event's misinformed socialites approached me and asked me if I'd help my author schedule some afternoon events in Park City for the following day. I'd had enough.

"I'm not a secretary, a sous-chef, nor a publicist. I'm a friend who drove out here to support another friend in his time of need. If you ask me to do one more administrative task that's not my responsibility because you poorly planned your damned party, I'm going to explode!"

Fact check: I'd already exploded.

"Stephanie, I'm so sorry. Micah told us you are his publicist."

"His... *huh*?"

And there we have it. For three weeks I had been beat up and bullied by entitled parties from coast to coast because of a simple word that was mispronounced.

"No. I'm a publisher. Not a publicist. I wouldn't even know the first thing about being a publicist and I have no intention to learn."

The woman's jaw dropped. "I'm so sorry. I was under a completely different impression."

The following day everybody who had bullied me to do a job I was unqualified for and uninterested in learning came up to me, one at a time, and apologized. I learned that the hostess had two dying family members and had just lost her husband. I learned that they had only one promotional partner follow through with their commitment. I learned that she was having panic attacks, crying once the house parties died down until the sun came up. We were all in over our heads, and it was all due to miscommunication. Lots and lots of it.

I couldn't stop thinking about "Dissidently Speaking" for the next several hours and the days that followed. Rather than rational engagement, honest discussion or problem solving, three phenomena Brent demystifies in this book, we were warring unnecessarily over misused words when we could or should have been embracing one another to make lemonade out of the lemons. It immediately struck me that this situation was an illustration of the very concepts Brent teaches in "Dissidently Speaking," and that all the pain, warring, division and judgment could have been avoided.

The most transformational moment during my Utah weekend was when a pink-haired self-proclaimed "shaman" approached me. I could sense her contrition as she had been one of the most adamant parties in badgering me to find money for the circus that was that Sundance event. In an instant,

I knew that she was the same as me; a victim of unnecessary word wars. We weren't only destined to hate one another at that party, but me being a straight-laced Christian and her being a passionate member of Team Rainbow, we were supposed to hate one another everywhere else, too.

Somehow I found the grace to look into her eyes and listen to her make conversation. We began to find common ground after fumbling around a bit. As she went on about her passion for so many political philosophies I found repugnant, I heard Brent in my head, "don't say what is. Just ask her, 'is it?'" This took the pressure off me to fight her to make my philosophy known. It freed up my energy to listen. And sure enough, by the end of the weekend, I found her to be the most delightful person at that party. I saw the beauty in her when I allowed her to be different, but still wonderful. We also found common ground on things I'd never expected us to agree on, such as certain promising elements of Orange Man and even her perspective on 9/11; topics that could have sealed the fate of our friendship irreparably and indefinitely. When, on the final day, she gave a musical performance with her partner at the event, I felt intoxicated with appreciation for her gifts and the beautiful human she is.

I arrived in Utah that weekend hellbent on hating several people. During the course of the event, I turned on my capacity to listen and love people while taking responsibility for my own inability to draw boundaries. I left feeling kinship and love for what I normally consider to be "the enemy," and was reminded that the real enemy is the pervasive, divisive language that separates us, prohibiting Americans from problem solving, at best, or leading us into much bigger wars than the two illustrated above, at worst.

This book isn't going to tell you who to vote for. It's not going to condemn you for your views on abortion, the Bible, nor any other "hot button issue." Not everybody reading this book needs more friends, needs to hug strangers, or needs to learn the art of drawing healthy boundaries. But everybody in America will surely benefit from being more intentional about language. By becoming better listeners. And by asking that important question, "is it?" in place of stating "it is."

With that I leave you with one of my absolute favorite passages from a beautifully written, well-crafted book by Brent Hamachek in "Dissidently Speaking," among the most intentional pieces I've read in seventeen years as a writer and avid reader.

The space between Team Right and Team Left in this country has become a sort of modern-American no man's land. Regular citizens don't know how to get there and our political and opinion leaders don't want you to go there. They want you to keep fighting. Let me suggest to you that it is time for a random act of civil disobedience. In defiance of your team platoon leaders, in defiance of your political leaders, in defiance perhaps of your own instincts, I implore you to step out of the trenches and don't go back in. Turn America's no man's land in to one of common ground.

Stephanie Pierucci
February, 2023

INTRODUCTION:

AN IDEA FOR ASSESSING
AMERICA 230+ YEARS IN

*"Nothing is more wonderful than the art of being free, but
nothing is harder to learn how to use than freedom."*
—Alexis de Tocqueville, *Democracy in America*

Where are we?

The nation that was created by our Founding Fathers in the latter part of the eighteenth century is commonly referred to as the "American experiment." I think that is the wrong framework in which to consider their design.

An experiment is the testing of a hypothesis. An individual or group sets the terms of the experiment, which then runs for a set time, sometimes in a controlled environment and sometimes in a natural one, and they have it commence. The results are then utilized either to create something or to launch the next experiment for which the last one was the required antecedent.

The only evidence that our forming was an experiment on the part of its designers is best summarized by Benjamin Franklin. When asked what kind of government had been formed, Franklin famously responded, "A republic, madam, if you can keep it." This suggests that Franklin and others knew that their design contained enough left to chance that it just might not ultimately work.

Not to quibble on semantics, but I believe there is a better way to evaluate America than that of characterizing it is an experiment. In order to use that paradigm, we have to logically say that the "experiment" has concluded and that results are in. Clearly, America has not "concluded." The fact that I sit at this moment typing a manuscript after having just signed my United States of America federal and state tax forms is proof that America continues. That said, the very fact that I signed a federal income tax form, something that did not exist when our nation was founded (as there was no national income tax), is one simple piece of evidence among hundreds upon thousands that our republic has dramatically changed.

How does an experiment keep changing without resetting the terms of the experiment? Doesn't it become a brand-new experiment the moment you introduce a new and previously unplanned variable? What sort of man-made vehicle changes constantly in order to continue to remain solvent or survive? The answer, which I can offer quite confidently after a 40-plus-year career as a privately owned business consultant, is that our republic is best thought of not as an experiment, but as a business.

As a business, our republic must continually adapt to our ever-changing customer base (citizens) and adjust to the actions of our competitors (other nations) in order to survive. We must continually reexamine our own corporate values, mission, and vision. Viewed in this context, we can see the formation of the United States of America back in 1787 (I choose the year the Constitution was drafted, but others could argue convincingly for 1775, 1776, 1788, or 1789) as being a new "Nation-State Business Startup," the Constitution being our "business plan."

What was the United States of America "selling" to its "customers" (read: citizens)? I suggest that the product or service (the metaphor is loose and either can be used) was an opportunity to live life under a deliberately constructed system that embraced Natural Law, specifically the English philosopher John Locke's (1656–1704) version of Natural Law that saw men forming a social contract so that there might be a fair and impartial way to mediate disputes over matters of life, liberty, and property. Locke's seminal writings on the topic came as the Age of Reason transitioned into the Enlightenment and it is he, among many but above all others, whose ideas I believe and assert most inspired our Founders.

America's ribbon-cutting was in September 1787, and who could have possibly imagined then what the fledgling "business" venture would look like today? Of course, there were concerns. Among them were Franklin's above-referenced warning, Madison's take on factions and the potential tyranny of the majority, and a host of others. But who could have seen where we are today? The question is rhetorical, but in its asking, there is help in proving the point that America is not best thought of as an experiment. Was there a hypothesis being tested? Some would argue yes. But I argue that more than any sort of an hypothesis, there was hope; hope that people would be willing and able to consume more individual liberty than had ever been offered in any nation-state prior to that time (or since, for that matter).

Here in the early twenty-first century, 236 years after the American startup as I type, the United States is still in business. Would our Founding Fathers recognize the company they started? It's an interesting question. To be sure they would recognize much of its structure. They would likely find pride in seeing that their construct of executive, legislative, and judicial branches has survived. They would most certainly be impressed that we have been able to expand from thirteen original states to fifty without having to jettison their work completely to accommodate the growth. Regarding amendments to the Constitution, we might get a mixed bag of responses, some happy to see so many (Jefferson, perhaps?), some disappointed for the same reason (Madison, perhaps?). If the Devil can cite Scripture for his purpose, historians and pundits certainly like to tell us what the Founding Fathers would have said today about a great many things. Anyone who has ever uttered the phrase to a close friend after tasting their latest cooking creation, "I can't believe you like it," should know the peril of assuming the thoughts of others, especially when those others are 200 years in the grave and lived in a radically different time.

How our Founding Fathers would react is as unknowable as knowing what Henry Ford might think of today's Ford Motor Company, or how George Westinghouse would consider the model of today's company that bears his name, or how Thomas Edison might feel about General Electric (a company from which he was fired by cofounder J. P. Morgan). Knowing their thoughts wouldn't help us much anyway, considering they are gone and we are here. A more productive endeavor might be to assess what "USA Inc." has produced over the past 200-plus years, how happy its clients are, and what that means for the future of the most powerful, prosperous, and free nation in history.

I won't stick with the business metaphor beyond this preface. To do so would run the risk of it feeling too trendy and unserious. I use it only as a way to frame thought as the reader travels through the writings that follow and to see this in the simple context of what *is* today is certainly not what *was* at the time of our origination. Think of what the United States of America has provided in real market data about a "freedom-based" service offering over the past couple of centuries. Here are some questions worth asking and my very quick takes on each (some are addressed in a more in-depth manner within these pages:

What happens to God in a free society? It appears that about a third of the people reject Him, about a third of the people weaponize Him, and another third try to hold to traditional understandings and truly worship Him.

The behavior exhibited by the respective members of the first two of these groups can be especially insidious. The nonbelievers often attempt to inhibit or prohibit the independent expression of faith by using the legal system to create church-state barriers never envisioned by our Founders. Within the second group, we have seen a whole financial opportunist class of "evangelists" emerge, some even claiming to be prophets, mesmerizing audiences with promises of salvation and political freedom if only they send them money through Apple Pay.

What have we learned about our nature and our ethics? It appears that people who are given freedom experience a violent collision between natural law and natural instincts. People tend to place a higher value on freedom for themselves than they do for others. Ethics are discussed in greater detail in Chapter 5.

How does law get administered and evolve? It becomes increasingly complex and nefariously used. We tend to think that every good idea needs to become a law, and like the child with the momentarily perfect drawing, we just can't stop coloring. We also come to understand that we can use the law to get things we want and punish those we don't like.

A vibrant example of this weaponization of law can be found in the headlines as I type this in the Christmas season of 2023. The Colorado Supreme Court has just ruled that Donald Trump cannot be on the ballot because he was part of an insurrection on January 6, 2021. As of this writing, the former president has been found guilty of no such crime. The Colorado justices have simply decreed his guilt. There can be no debate as to the unconstitutionality of their action. Yet there is debate. America has succeeded in turning black letters into primitive cave drawings subject to capricious interpretation.

This leads us to the great paradox of law for a free people: *We need to have a great many laws because of the harm we will do to each other absent restrictions. At the same time, we need very few laws because we cannot trust either the people who make them or those who enforce them.*

How does free market capitalism adapt and evolve? It does its very best when it is engaged in the process of discovering and inventing. Once things are invented, however, free people don't always use the new capability in the best of ways. It has created and delivered the tools that bring us great comfort, and it has created and delivered the tools (some of the same tools) currently used to control us. It is still, however, the best possible system because it disperses self-interest, thereby making it harder for the few to effectively use their self-interest to control the many.

How does political activity get organized? Read the chapter following this one. You will learn all about how political teams take the "team: out of teamwork.

Is there a way to control citizenship and entry? There is, but the wealthier a nation becomes, the less it has the willingness to do so. There are a number of forces at work that lead to this sort of paralysis. For the general population, a lack of desire to control borders likely stems from the combination of guilt and its favorite carry-on travel companion, obligation. We feel guilty about our historically unparalleled standard of living, so we feel obligated to let others share in the experience, regardless of consequences.

From a leadership perspective, there are more nefarious reasons for not controlling entry into the country. Retention of power, access to cheaper labor, and a deliberate move toward primarily being a subservient member of a global community versus that of a strong sovereign nation state top the list.

Can a free country conduct itself in foreign affairs in a manner consistent with its values? The answer here seems to be a resounding and unequivocal "no." While the United States has done much good in the world, especially up to and through World War II, its more recent actions are difficult to defend. A nation can make mistakes in foreign policy, but when it comes behaving in a manner consistent with your values, it kind of needs to bat 100 percent. You can easily make the argument that since the end of World War II, the United States has been the most failed nation *of consequence* in modern history. We didn't allow the rise of China as a superpower; we facilitated it. We didn't inherit instability in the Middle East; we created it. We didn't get blindsided by Russian expansion into Ukraine; we effectively backed them into it. It is no longer even remotely possible to overlay U.S. foreign misadventures with the guiding principles of our constitution. Our Foreign policy decisions have, for the most part, been made by leaders acting like they have a pocket filled with tokens playing in the Devil's arcade. Those tokens coming in the form of American lives and treasure.

What effect does technology have, especially with regard to communication? It has provided for a standard of living unparalleled in human history and unequaled anywhere else in the world. It has also, unfortunately, taken the personal out of personal communication and made it too easy for people to hate in the third person—hating the "theys" and "thems." It has also made it very easy for minority-size factions to form and cause disruption, something James Madison specifically dismissed in his time. This was a pure "miss" on Madison's part as he believed the majority could contain the minority. History, however, has long been shaped and moved by well-focused minorities.

So big was Madison's miss that it actually could ultimately be the undoing of our Republic should we collapse. It was back in 1945 that philosopher Karl Popper in his notes to his work *The Open Society and Its Enemies* identified what he called the "paradox of tolerance." In short summary, Popper's paradox, put in the form of question, was could a free society survive when it is forced to tolerate minority (defined only numerically, not by race or any other characteristic) factions that are intolerant? Madison would have said most certainly they could because the majority could just assert itself. In twenty-first-century America, we can clearly see that this is not the case. Virtually all the threats to our individual liberty have emanated from the actions of intolerant minority factions.

Why we have allowed this to happen can be found in a strange elixir of manners, negligence, altruism, apathy, guilt, and all sorts of other attributes that have led to a repudiation of our duties as Americans assigned to safeguard liberty. Is it too late? Keep reading.

And perhaps most interestingly:

How did our original business plan, the Constitution, hold up over time? Relatively well, owing in large part to the conflict between having the ability to amend it, but not having the ability to do so easily. Were our Founders here today, they might have wanted to either clarify, or outright eliminate, the Commerce Clause, based upon its use to radically expand the reach and authority of the federal government. They also might think they needed to better address the kind of inherent conflict between the Supremacy Clause (federal law trumps any contrary state law) and the Tenth Amendment (all non-enumerated powers are left to the states). They didn't envision so many federal laws that would greatly impair states' rights.

They also could never have anticipated the ability to travel and communicate so easily, quickly, and universally. James Madison specifically mentioned our vast geographic territory as an inhibitor of the ability to form factions. Technology has removed the impediment.

All are obviously free to provide your own answers to those questions, but I encourage you to at least contemplate them.

COMPOSING *DISSIDENTLY SPEAKING*

In this book, I have assembled a series of essays, all previously published and composed over the course of eight years. Any one piece could be ordered first, last, or anywhere in between. Everything is, on some level, interrelated, and I will attempt to show the connectivity wherever possible and whenever I, myself, realize it to be present. I say that because a discerning reader might well find threads that I've missed. I write this with no misconception that I know all or see all. I write about that which I believe, I know, and think I see.

I noted that I believe that John Locke was the most influential of all the intellectuals who helped to shape the ideas of our Founding Fathers. There are many others. Montesquieu and Cicero instantly come to mind as two who had a great influence on the structure of the Constitution. The great English jurist and legal scholar William Blackstone certainly had an impact, especially in the drafting of the Declaration of Independence, which, if properly read, is really a very well-written and thorough legal complaint against the English monarchy. In stopping there, I fall far short of the full pantheon of minds, but the point of this exercise is not to identify all of the influencers from over two thousand years who impacted our Founders and to what extent. The objective is to look at where we started and what we have learned. That said, there is one great thinker of the seventeenth century who most certainly had an influence, although he is not cited as being behind our founding. That man is the English father of social contract theory, the ever-present Thomas Hobbes (1588–1679), the author of the classic *Leviathan*.

Because Hobbes is so influential on my thinking, and because each of the entries in this book was at one time a stand-alone piece, you will find many references to Hobbes and with some amount of redundancy. I have deliberately not altered that because I hope that through redundancy I will spark curiosity for the previously unaware to dig deeper and learn more about this remarkably insightful and influential thinker from the seventeenth century.

Legend has it that Hobbes (he gets regular mentions in these pages) was born prematurely as his mother was forced into panicked labor at the thought of the Spanish Armada off the coast of England. It is said that Hobbes, being born in a burst of fear, had his dark perceptions of man indelibly etched in his mind prior to the cord being cut. Contemporary knowledge of neuroscience makes difficult the belief of such conjecture, but regardless of causes, Hobbes came to believe that the nature of man was, well, somewhat dark. In *Leviathan*, he creates what is called social contract theory, a hypothetical moment where mankind decides it is going to surrender its self-governing state of anarchy and submit to an authority. Hobbes's well-known description of life for man in the pre–social contract state of nature is that of being, "solitary, poor, nasty, brutish, and short." That's the quote everyone knows, but there is more; much more. Hobbes also had this to say about man's nature:

The right of nature... is the liberty each man hath to use his own power, as he will himself, for the preservation of his own nature; that is to say, of his own life.

And this . . .

During the time men live without a common power to keep them all in awe, they are in that condition called war; and such a war, as if of every man, against every man.

Compare those sentiments against those of the aforementioned Locke in describing man's natural state:

The state of nature has a law of nature to govern it, which obliges every one: and reason, which is that law, teaches all mankind, who will but consult it, that being all equal and independent, no one ought to harm another in his life, health, liberty, or possessions.

Or this . . .

To love our neighbor as ourselves is such a truth for regulating human society, that by that alone one might determine all the cases in social morality.

These are not congruous assessments of who and what men are. If Locke was the one who inspired our Founders to give men the liberty and freedom to which they aspire, Hobbes was the one tapping them on the shoulder and admonishing them to ignore his assessments at their own peril.

As I mentioned above, this collection is not intended to go into detail on the various philosophers who influenced our Founders. It is also not intended, despite the above emphasis, to go into a detailed description of the differences between the philosophies of Locke and Hobbes. I encourage all to read their works in their original form (Locke an easy read, Hobbes torturous) and come to their own opinions. I have compiled this collection of thoughts because I genuinely believe that our Founders had Locke sitting on one shoulder and Hobbes sitting upon the other. One whispering sweet, inspirational sounds, the other grimacing and sneering, "just go ahead and try to let men be free . . . You'll see." My intent is to help shine light upon which of the ideas of those two great minds seem to be prevailing in today's America, Inc. I'll leave it to the reader to decide.

One thing is for certain: Had the nauseating contemporary business analysis term "SWOT" analysis been *en vogue* in 1787 (Strengths, Weaknesses, Opportunities, Threats), our Founders would definitely have had both Hobbes and Locke notes on their quill-penned whiteboard.

I will refer to these two great minds occasionally throughout the text but not incessantly. Again, they set the premise for how we view the American business model, knowing that the disagreement in their conceptualizations impacted our Founders. In looking at America's journey from today's perspective, to use a tasty metaphor, were America a wishbone with both Hobbes and Locke pulling, who seems to have had the larger segment clasped in their hand upon breaking?

A RIGHT TO WRITE . . .

In academic circles, those in which I will likely be roundly criticized and dismissed for writing this book owing to what they might consider a lack of credentialing, the ultimate insult to anyone's contribution is to say that the work is "derivative." That is to say, the work lacks original thought and simply builds upon the work of others prior. This is a sort of empty critique insofar as, on some level, all works are derivative. I always start my private tutoring with someone by suggesting that there are two things true of all political theorists. The first is that all of them are right about something. The second is that each and every one of them is a product of their own subjective experiences, everything that has ever happened before them, and the time and place in which they live.

My self-confessed source of my derivations stems from having spent forty years in the world of business (something for which I will not criticize academics for failing to have experienced), a lifetime of self-directed study, and a ten-year run of writing and speaking on the kinds of topics that are addressed within these pages. Indeed, the entire content of this book is derivative in the sense that I have derived it from previously published pieces of my own. My assessments of the American experience are unique to the extent that they arise from my having drawn my own conclusions. To the point that they might be shared by others, I simply say that it gives me some sense of validation. Many of the themes found herein are ones I have shared in either writings or lectures, often to an audience's strong disagreement. That I always welcome. I do not profess to be the smartest person in any room or on any keyboard.

A quick note on being the "smartest person in the room." I was once asked by a young professional how it was that I seemed to do so well in negotiating when I was typically out-positioned and overmatched in terms of professional status or personal wealth. My answer was and is, "You don't have to be the smartest person in the room. You just have to remember that nobody in the room is as smart as they think they are. *That* is their weakness!"

I do hope that if people take issue with what I write, it will be based upon rational disagreements with my conclusions and not because of some jaundiced eye view of my CV. If you think I am wrong, then think so because of my reasoning, not because of a perception that I'm not qualified to reason. I welcome meritorious challenges. I reply to every email sent to Brent@BrentHamachek.com.

During the pandemic, I reached out to a professor at a highly respected "conservative" university and asked him if he would do an interview with me to discuss the ethical decisions and dilemmas posed by the lockdown. He replied that the idea was a good one but that an interview with me would be a waste of time because he would have to spend too much time explaining things to me. That sort of condescension is a problem in academia and a reason why everyday people cannot necessarily find the ideas of the greatest minds readily available to them to read in understandable, actionable language.

This creates the question of whether or not academics should stay out of the real world. It is my belief that what tends to happen when academics teach students (who ultimately enter the real world unless they, too, become academics), those students then take only fragments of what they were taught into the world and start to apply them in parts, heuristically, and that can lead to a lot of misunderstandings over ideas. The best example of this is Karl Marx, the famous philosopher who everybody references and nobody actually reads. Marx's ideas have been misapplied, misused, and misunderstood almost since the day he created them. Academics could help fix that. They need to do better. Ideas need to be properly understood, and they do matter. As the Scottish philosopher Thomas Carlisle said, "There was once a man called Rousseau who wrote a book containing nothing but ideas. The second edition was bound in the skins of those who had laughed at the first."

Referring back to my business career, it is without question that my opportunity to work in the "real world" as an active observer not just of behavior, but of the American experience in general, has greatly informed my opinions. Seeing how people act in hundreds upon hundreds of different situations is very different than just simply thinking about how they should or shouldn't act. I have spent forty years asking myself questions like, "What am I really seeing here? Why are they doing this? What are the environmental factors driving and permitting this attitude and behavior?" These are questions that just don't get asked and answered the same way if all we have available is Descartes's reason. I had empirical observation to supplement and stimulate thought. This is the culmination of all those experiences.

A NEW AMERICAN
OPERATING AGREEMENT

We're left then with the question of purpose. Why compile this book? This is complex for me as for a long time I have used terminology that contends America is "going out of business." That language stems from my extensive background in turnaround work where you can clearly see the signs of a company that just isn't going to make it. Given the division present in this country in 2024, a division like that of the Civil War, materially different only because the battle lines are not drawn geographically but, instead, around dining room tables, it is easy to say that the country is no longer salvageable. Many people share that thought publicly, some going so far as to suggest on the mild side that states partition into two separate red-blue countries, while others call for all-out revolution. I don't believe that either of those things will happen, and I no longer believe that American is going out of business per se.

In terms of partitioning states, there have been many who have put a great deal of thought into this. Maps can be found that draw the various boundaries and descriptions of governance and shared responsibilities that could potentially work. As a practical matter, and I mean practical matter, it can't ever possibly work. First, for a nation to be so divided that it agrees to split it will not by definition be able to agree as to how to split. Two sides need to have so much vitriol for each other to get to this point that material agreement cannot be reached. This falls apart instantly just on the single issue of national (continental) defense: *Who shall risk whose life for what, and who shall pay for it?*

In partitioning states, there would also be the problem of massive citizen unrest because not 100 percent of the residents of New York are collectivists and not 100 percent of the citizens of Florida are individualists. The immense disruption caused by dividing states would lead to even more hostility than is evidenced almost everywhere today in our private and civic lives. I would say that the idea is fun to kick around in theory, but I actually think the opposite. The idea is dangerous because it diverts people's attention away from rational and possibly problem-solving concepts.

Regarding a revolution, here is why I do not believe it is going to happen, although I have many friends who believe it to be not just possible, but likely. We are living in this particular moment in time in the most opulent and comfortable society ever seen in all of human history. I mean right in this exact moment. Say what you want about imperfections, inequalities, those who are suffering, etc. The truth is that the poorest among us, save for the homeless, typically have cars, flat screen televisions, air-conditioning, and of course most important, smartphones. Now, in order for there to be revolution, you need some perfect elixir of anger (check), mixed with both a feeling that you have really nothing left to lose and that you can prevail in the revolt. Think of it in terms of an equation:

Revolution = (Desperation + Hope) x Anger

It is hope of success that creates the biggest problem. In our first revolution, fought in the days of muskets, cannons, and knives, there was a much greater chance for the colonists being able to prevail. Today, given the extraordinary weaponry of the state, winning a revolution is much more difficult and would certainly result in more dramatic loss of life (that is, assuming that state-weaponized agents were willing to fire upon their own people, something that history suggests is not an impossible desire to rally). With the likelihood of success a bit lower, that means you need to increase the amount of desperation. Here we return to the physical comfort enjoyed by even the poorest among us in this, the wealthiest of all possible nations. The likelihood of revolution starts to decrease rapidly.

Making the equation all the more complicated is that "Anger" may not be (in fact, it likely is not) a truly independent variable. Anger can get increased or decreased by changes in the factors of desperation and hope for success, potentially causing the multiplier in the model to simultaneously shrink as the two other variables shrink. A mathematician would rightly note that this is a flaw in the formula. Exactly. I agree, and that is why I believe the calculation that revolution is on the horizon is incorrect. It's bad sociological math.

What I believe to be the case is this: The business plan for the original United States of America startup is getting to be almost unrecognizable in our country's daily affairs. What will emerge is a country (or company to sit with the metaphor a bit longer) with a far more collectivist-based operating model. I do not see a ready way to reverse this for reasons that I will touch upon, either directly or inferentially, throughout the remainder of the book. Writing from the biased position of a long-time individualist, I regret this inescapable reality. Said simply, I love Locke and recognize Hobbes.

GOALS FOR THIS BOOK

Back to why am I writing this. It is my hope that this book becomes my contribution to simply making people aware of where we are and how we got here. If that can be understood, then freedom-loving individualists might be ready to find ways to contribute to not so much reversing course, but in reinserting Natural Law–based liberties. In yet another metaphor (I have a great fondness for them), if the American business model were a 747 jumbo jet, it is getting ready to crash. As a pilot, I have two options: I can nosedive the plane into the ground, certainly killing everyone on board instantly, or I can look for the best place to land, warn the passengers, and do my best to create survivors. Those survivors can then help others through triage and treatment. This is my attempt to try and help land the plane.

It does us no good as Americans to get emotional about where we are. Emotions cloud rational judgment and prevent reasoned action. This does not mean we should be dispassionate. It means we should be passionate about following rational prescriptions for action. The time for that informed rational action is right now because that "plane" has dropped well below the Natural Law hard deck.

One of the most destructive notions ever adopted by free people is that everything is cyclical. Like its corollary, "The pendulum swings both ways," this sort of notion becomes a self-medicating form of mass social delusion. It allows people to sit back and think that whatever is today will simply be reversed tomorrow. This is foolhardy. It lulls people into a false sense of security because they think that if they just wait long enough, things will go back to where they were. They won't, not unless somebody picks them up and carries them. We live in a world of cause-and-effect, one that is governed by trajectory and velocity. The directionality of the United States should be clear at this point, and if it isn't already, perhaps reading this book will help you see the missile's path.

In support of my contention that cyclical notions are fallacious, I want to give you a different way to view our history with a focus on individual liberty. If you "measure" the idea of individual liberty the way I do, which is to say having the minimal amount of interference from legislative rules impacting your daily life, I believe that we have been seeing that individual liberty eroding over the past 100-plus years. The slide at first was gradual, but of late, it has been taken away at an increasing rate.

In defense of that statement, I offer what I call the American Liberty Timeline:

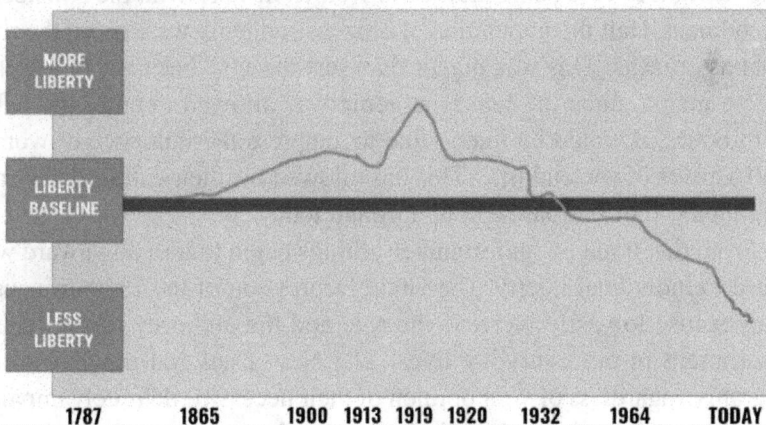

American Liberty Timeline

MORE LIBERTY

LIBERTY BASELINE

LESS LIBERTY

1787   1865   1900 1913 1919 1920   1932   1964   TODAY

I start with 1787, the year the Constitution was drafted, as a baseline. If I am going to try to objectively measure something with a good deal of subjectivity, it is important that I have something defined as a baseline, a sort of ground zero. What better place than at the moment of our creation? If I am going to argue that things are getting worse (or better, as you will see), it is right to ask, worse or better than what?" Seventeen eighty-seven was the year our Founders decided how much liberty to give us, and they gave us more than any people of any nation had heretofore been granted.

I argue that we stayed relatively close along that baseline until 1865, when we constitutionally emancipated slaves. You cannot argue that all other things being equal, eliminating the ability for one human being to own another does not drastically increase the amount of individual liberty. It doesn't mean any other problems associated with slavery and its legacy were instantly fixed. It just means people couldn't legally own people anymore. In 1865, we move above the baseline.

In the early 1900s, however, we start to track south. There are a number of factors for this. One is the beginning of a more imperial presidency under Theodore Roosevelt, who began to more fully wield the power of the Executive branch. Another was the introduction of a federal income tax along with the creation of the Federal Reserve System to centralize banking authority. Power was beginning to move from the various states, where it was dispersed and fragmented, and toward Washington, where it could be consolidated. This would continue uninterrupted right through this present day.

We did, however, get one last major springboard for individual liberty with the right to vote being granted to women in 1919 with the Nineteenth Amendment. Half the population of citizens suddenly were given the right to act as citizens. This was bigger than just the vote because, in a sort of reverse magic, once the feminine genie was allowed to enter the ballot booth bottle, it would be impossible to suppress the influence of women in all aspects of societal life. This has allowed for their extraordinary and continuous contributions right up through today.

From that point on, unfortunately, things begin to turn downward with regard to individual liberty. The Great Depression of the 1930s was used as an excuse to vastly increase the role and the authority of the federal government in our everyday lives. The New Deal and other resulting programs, regardless of your opinion of their necessity, definitely impaired individual liberty defined as limited control over our daily actions by government. I will explain more about this as a process in Chapter 1.

The 1960s and the Great Society programs created more of what Roosevelt and the New Deal started. Again, I will abstain from critiquing the merits of these programs, but by definition, they limited individual liberty.

A digression is in order to allow me to defend in advance a criticism I know is forthcoming for my having equated large federal government relief and transfer programs with limitations on individual liberty. I know that some will argue that these programs, by helping some at the expense of others, allow for those being helped to enjoy greater individual liberty. In defense of my position that these programs, while perhaps desirable and beneficial, do in fact reduce individual liberty, I turn to the man some consider the father of sociology, William Graham Sumner, a professor at Yale University in the late nineteenth and early twentieth centuries.

Sumner created the concept of the "Forgotten Man," a phrase that FDR took for himself and twisted its use during the Depression. In writing in an 1883 essay, Sumner said this:

As soon as A observes something which seems to him to be wrong, from which X is suffering, A talks it over with B, and A and B then propose to get a law passed to remedy the evil and help X. Their law always proposes to determine what C shall do for X or, in the better case, what A, B and C shall do for X. As for A and B, who get a law to make themselves do for X what they are willing to do for him, we have nothing to say except that they might better have done it without any law, but what I want to do is to look up C. I want to show you what manner of man he is. I call him the Forgotten Man. Perhaps the appellation is not strictly correct. He is the man who never is thought of. He is the victim of the reformer, social speculator and philanthropist, and I hope to show you before I get through that he deserves your notice both for his character and for the many burdens which are laid upon him.

Using Sumner's construct, I would argue that a great many Americans have been forgotten over the past century and their liberty has been diminished in the process.

In yet another aside (I enjoy digressions), Sumner's "Forgotten Man" illustrates the essentially unsolvable math problem of unrestricted illegal entry into the country. Forget your opinions about what our obligations are ethically (much more on ethics later in this book) to permit entry into the United States, the problem is one of calculating maximum load capabilities are that can be handled by person C. Consider the following:

CBS News reported that in December 2023, there were over 200,000 illegal crossings into the United Sates at the southern border. This is roughly the same number of new jobs that were reported by the U.S. Department of Labor as being created in the same month. Now remember that there are roughly 330 million of us in the United States to begin with, and further keep in mind that technology is continuing to eliminate the need to hire workers in virtually every aspect of employment.

Here is the math problem in words. In mathematics there is something known as a transfer function—something that shows the impact from an input to an output. Since it is very unlikely that the United States can create enough new jobs to sustain the inflow of new entrants into the country, some significant percentage of those people will have to become reliant upon federal and state assistance. A and B will want to "do the right thing" by them, and so they will turn to C in order to take-from for the purpose of giving-to. If C had a fixed amount to take to begin with, this would be a problem in and of itself, but it is worse than that. Because of changing circumstances in employment, both from technological advancement and a rapidly increasing pool of labor through immigration, C is going to have less to take. C will eventually collapse. The inputs of millions entering our country are going to crash C's output.

Another name for C is what we term imprecisely, but with a general understanding, the middle class. It has already taken an incredible beating in this country but this rapidly growing influx of X's might just be what eventually is ruled its cause of death. To borrow a fancied term from our times, it certainly is not sustainable.

Since the 1960s, we have seen an increase of government presence dictating the "cans" and "can'ts" of everyday life, right up to the time of the pandemic, when we saw an explosion of liberty-restricting rules in a way we had never seen before in our history.

Regarding our history, there have been numerous attempts of late to try to "erase" or change it. This can be seen in the removal of statues, the renaming of everything from holidays, to venues, to city streets. There have even been deliberate omissions from school texts of key historical events and figures. This attempt to erase history is more nefarious than a simple act of virtue signaling or political correctness carried too far. There is a darker force at work.

I sometimes play a game with an audience where I take my right hand, index finger pointed, drop it to my side and across my body to the left, and then gradually raise it up and across toward the ceiling. I stop abruptly, and while frozen, I ask the audience in which direction my finger is traveling. Everyone correctly indicates upward to the right. I next announce that we are going to start over. I then take my right index finger and simply point it at them. I ask in what direction my arm is traveling. The audience rightly shrugs.

It is our history, all of our history, that not only shows direction but can show where we are in relation to from where we have come. Alter history, erase history, then there is no context for a nation's place. It is anywhere and nowhere. This is the goal of critical theory, to remove the absolute, in this case history, and replace it with the relatively defined. This is quite dangerous insofar as while you might be able over time to erase an understanding of history, you can't erase history itself. It *was* and we *are* as a result of it. It must be left in place, fully embraced (both good and bad) and used as a way to chart our course and see where we are heading.

HISTORY DOESN'T REPEAT ITSELF

Here is the good news: History doesn't repeat itself (the shortened and corrupted version of George Santayana's quote: "Those who do not remember the past are condemned to repeat it"; there is much truth in that). If it did, we would always know what is going to happen next. We don't. Ebeneezer Scrooge asked the last spirit if he was seeing the future that would be or that might be. We have every opportunity to alter our future. Not to reverse course, but to alter trajectory. We can become causes and not just effects. Just because moments of freedom in past times have been episodic and extinguished, it doesn't mean that ours has to be.

It is critical to understand that most of recorded human history has been lived under circumstances where the few or the one ruled oppressively over the many. Always the general ratio has the measure of many more serfs than masters. What this suggests is that while it may be man's desire to be free, perhaps that is something only aspirational and not truly natural? If that is the case, it makes the "business" our Founding Fathers tried to launch even more difficult to sustain. Natural Law might just be Romanticized Law? This doesn't mean we should surrender its idea. It simply means we must fight harder, perhaps even fight our own nature, to keep it alive and allow it to function.

The United States as a landmass isn't going anywhere. One of the reasons people like to invest in real estate is because of its physical permanence. The lot at the corner of State and Main will always be. What can change about that permanent lot is the general public's assessment as to what is its highest and best use. Commercial? Residential? Industrial? What we are waiting to have determined, or perhaps fighting to help determine, is how the physical piece of real estate labeled as the United States of America is going to be "zoned" for use.

Our geological fixed presence, guarded by our physical isolation provided by two oceans, means we have every chance and likelihood of continuing. What might that come to mean?

Let us start within these pages by looking at what it has meant. To do so, we have to travel over 200 years to get to the present. This collection of writings will present a little bit of history, a little bit of sociology, a little bit of psychology, a little bit of political science, and a great deal of challenges. Challenges to what, you might ask? I intend to challenge your preconceived notions about the nation, about others, and about yourself. Above all, after reading my thoughts on the divisions within America today, if I have one hope for the reader, it is this:

That you flip two words in your lexicon and turn the declarative into the interrogative. I hope that you might stop saying "it is" as has become the norm in America today and replace the phrase with "is it?"

If that can happen on a wide scale, then, yes, we can change the world. We can certainly alter the trajectory of the country. You will hear that phrase again within these pages.

Three more notes before proceeding further. As already mentioned, this is a collection of previously published works, all updated from their original form, that were written for different purposes and in different times. As a result, there might be a certain lack of cadence to them. Try to look beyond the lack of clear sequencing and view the collection as an art gallery with different rooms featuring different styled works but all revolving around a general theme. Perhaps this could be thought of as the literary gallery of the American business?

Also, it is important for me to again make clear that I write from the perspective of someone who deeply believes in the ideal of individual liberty and voluntary, non-coerced action among all people. That means I abhor central planning and collective decision-making and edicts. Socialism (centralized planning, management, and oversight of political, social, and economic activity) is not my friend. So when I stray from observation to commentary, I do so with a fully disclosed preference. That said, because I believe in the non-coercive selling of ideas instead of the compulsion to adhere to them, I hope to only open readers' minds so that, at some point, I might be able to persuade, never compel, them to see the benefits and morality contained in a society that promotes individualism over collectivism.

And finally, I invite the reader to pause in between each essay to allow the theories presented to settle in. Notice the ways in which your thoughts and language patterns begin to change, or at least how much more carefully you choose your responses based upon the ideas and challenges in these four unique parts. The book isn't designed to be read cover to cover in a night. Rather, aim to read one essay weekly. Once you finish an essay, take the time to reflect and even to journal on the material for that week. Treat this book as a course in elevating your thoughts and language.

Above all, be patient with yourself as the concepts in this book are intended to undo so many "bad habits" we have all subconsciously adopted over years or, more likely, decades of regular use. Many neuroscientists believe it takes between two and six months to rewire a single thought. In this sense, I hope that the reader will take their time to allow each essay's ideas to be consecrated, even if that means devoting the entire year to the valiant work of elevating one's discourse or, in some cases, learning when *not* to engage. Sometimes, even when you win an argument, you lose. With the tools in this book, you will find as many reasons not to engage in discourse that would previously trigger yourself and another party as you will to engage in a revolutionized form of conversation. Remember, my ultimate goal is for us to stop saying, "it is" and to begin asking, "is it?" Not only is this a tool to diffuse otherwise needlessly heated or discriminatory conversations, but it's a tool that will, in effect, bring more compassion and equanimity to most interactions.

Having worked with numerous individuals in writing books, I always start a project by asking this question: When the reader has finished your book and closed the cover for the final time, what do you want them to do next? It is only sporting that in this solo project I ask myself the same question.

In attempting to answer, I will share this thought with all of you who are of the mind to believe that you need to share lots of facts with those around you to get them to understand the challenges we face as a nation. While facts are important things, and while in an upcoming chapter, I will discuss them in great detail, the simple fact about facts is this: There are an overwhelming number of them, and inundating anybody with them as a means by which to convince them of something can easily cause them to feel overwhelmed.

Think of facts like data being input into a computer, and think of the brain as that computer's central processing unit. You can have all sorts of amazing data, but if the CPU isn't able to handle it all, the computer will crash. If the CPU can have its capacity for receiving data expanded and its processing capability to process the data improved, then it can easily handle any number of inputs, separate valid data from invalid, and come to better conclusions. It is my intention with this work to help to expand and improve everyone's personal CPU so that you are better equipped to process all the data (facts) that inundate you in this, the (dis)information age. I believe that the key to enhancing anyone's neural CPU is the introduction of ideas.

This is ultimately a book of ideas, and here is what I would like you, the reader, to do if you manage to struggle through this work . . .

I want you to think!

Some years ago, my good friend, Tom Kuchan, and I had the opportunity to teach an extension course for the Graduate School of Banking at the University of Wisconsin. As former bankers who had become successful outside of banking, we thought it would be helpful to commercial bankers to share what we had learned. The purpose was to show them the tricks that businesspeople use to fool them.

Our course was not successful.

The feedback we got from GSB staff was that bankers liked lists of things. We didn't have a list. As a result, our content was lost upon attendees.

In that spirit, I have a list of five things I want you to contemplate and remember as you read through this text:

1. Turn the declarative into the interrogative. Stop saying *it is* and start asking *is it*.
2. Learn to discern. Become a healthy skeptic.
3. Internalizing beats memorizing. Focus on how you process the facts you have, not on maximizing the number of facts you can recite.
4. Remember that history does not repeat itself, but human nature is constant.
5. If you are concerned about the direction in which our country is heading, remember we need converts; not casualties. Evangelize but don't terrorize.

For those who like lists, I hope you find that helpful as you continue on through these pages with me.

Ps. Anyone who knows me is well aware that I am a big fan of the greatest singer/songwriter/ performer of all-time, Bruce Springsteen. This wouldn't be my book without a tip of the hat to "The Boss." Accordingly, in every chapter, the discerning Springsteen aficionado will find a fragment of a lyric tucked away somewhere. Enjoy the hunt. If you already finished this introduction, did you catch it?

I'm known for saying, "there's a Springsteen song for everything." That applies even to my own work. There isn't any point in writing a book filled with serious ideas if you can't have a little fun and get a little lost along the way. Since I'm about to warn you that there is a darkness on the edge of town that threatens our very American skin, it's important to remember that most of us were born in the USA, we take care of our own, and we are all tougher than the rest. We've got this!

PROMPTS FOR REFLECTION: WHAT'S YOUR TAKE?

What happens to God in a free society?

_____

_____

_____

_____

_____

What have we learned about our nature and our ethics?

_____

_____

_____

_____

_____

How does law get administered and evolve?

_____

_____

_____

_____

_____

How does free market capitalism adapt and evolve?

_____

_____

_____

_____

_____

How does political activity get organized?

_____

_____

_____

_____

_____

Is there a way to control citizenship and entry?

_____

_____

_____

_____

_____

Can a free country conduct itself in foreign affairs in a manner consistent with its values?

_____

_____

_____

_____

_____

What effect does technology have, especially with regard to communication?

_____

_____

_____

_____

_____

How did our original business plan, the Constitution, hold up over time?

_____

_____

_____

_____

_____

CHAPTER ONE:

AN IDEA FOR ENDING OUR NATIONAL DIVISION

"But if thought corrupts language, language can also corrupt thought."
—George Orwell, *1984*

SYMPTOMS OF A NATIONAL BEHAVIORAL AND LANGUAGE DISORDER[1]

The eminent historian Will Durant once wrote the following:

"If you wish to converse with me," said Voltaire, "define your terms." How many a debate would have been deflated into a paragraph if the disputants had dared to define their terms! This is the alpha and omega of logic, the heart and soul of it: that every important term in serious discourse shall be subjected to strictest scrutiny and definition. It is difficult, and ruthlessly tests the mind; but once done it is half of any task.

Durant's postulate, leveraging Voltaire, goes right to the heart of what divides America today. To be sure, we have real and serious differences in need of debate and resolution. The problem is that we cannot even begin to address them because we disagree over terms. We are using the wrong ones in the wrong way with the intention of vilifying others.

I am about to take your political toy box, filled with terms and ideas, and dump it all over the floor. It is going to get intellectually uncomfortable. If you are currently wearing a piece of jewelry that you never remove, I ask you to remove it and set it on the table beside you. Physically parting

---

1 Originally Titled: "How America Broke Its Wings—The Causes and Effects of the Right-Left Divide and How to Repair It." (Turning Point USA, 2015)

with an object of comfort might prepare you to set aside ideas that you've found just as reassuring.

Might I add that looking at things differently does not necessarily require making the uncomfortable admission that you were wrong about something. At my age, I remember having owned and worn a light blue leisure suit in the 1970s. While I no longer sport that look, I have no regrets over the wide lapels and the flared legs. I have simply evolved in my view of fashion.

It is time to evolve in our views about the American political paradigm and its attendant dynamics.

Anyone, regardless of their level of education or the context in which they are communicating, who uses the terms "right-left" to describe the American political paradigm does so at best recklessly and ignorantly, and at worst deliberately and maliciously with the intention of trying to create division and stir conflict. If I have just labeled your favorite commentator, professor, or politician in a derogatory manner and have offended you, so be it. Keep reading. The terms are without any agreed-upon meaning and are simple pejoratives that we use to simplify what is actually already a quite simple structure if we would just take the time to understand it.

When I lecture on this topic, I open with a series of slides that depict two well-known political figures side-by-side. While I vary the actual people I choose based upon the current times, the approach is always the same. I show two people who are both associated as being right or left, juxtapose them, and then ask the audience to tell me who is farther right or left.

One common figure who I like to use is Kentucky Republican Senator Rand Paul. Paul is considered by many to be the most libertarian (very minimal government) high-ranking member of the Republican Party. A very usual first slide I will present is that of Senator Paul alongside Republican Senator Ted Cruz. I then ask the audience, "Who is farther right?"

I always get a mixed show of hands, usually with a majority tending to choose Senator Paul. When I ask an audience member why they chose Cruz, often the reason centers around his abortion stance and his commitment to religious faith. Conversely, when asked why they chose Paul, the typical response is because of his strong stand on limited government.

Hmm?

I continue with a couple of more slides that usually zero in on Senator Paul next to another known "right-winger." Paul usually gets the majority of a show of hands against each opponent, the explanation continuing to be his libertarian views.

Then I shock the audience. I put up a slide of Senator Paul next to Adolph Hitler and ask the audience again which of the two is farther right. Interestingly, instead of the audience being split, most do not even raise their hands to vote. They realize that they have just been logically trapped and they do not know what to do about it. Anyone who had been voting for Senator Paul in previous slides as being farther right because of his libertarian views realizes, at least intuitively, that if they put Senator Paul farther to the right than Adolph Hitler, what do they do with Hitler? Where does he go?

The content that follows will explain where Hitler goes, where Paul goes, and more importantly, it will explain where all of us go and how we operate politically.

I call what I'm offering a theory in the true scientific method sense of the word. It has both predictive and explanatory use, and it can be tested repeatedly and corroborated in the real world. When you think you might find exceptions to it (and we will point some of those out), you will find that upon closer examination, those "exceptions" are actually proving the rule.

We are a nation obsessed with labels. A Google search of the Hamachek family name with a hyphen and then the word "peas" after it will reveal a fascinating bit of trivia about my family lineage. It was a member of my father's family who was an early pioneer of the pea-vining machine. My father, born in 1912, told a story of working in the pea-canning plant as a young boy. He said that the canning process would be running (quite labor intensive, he recalled) and then they would hear a horn blow and production would stop. They would change the labels to read "Premium Peas" instead of just plain peas. They would then start up production again.

The label changed but the peas didn't. Oh, what people will believe when they read it on a label.

When I first wrote this essay back in early 2015, I opened it with a variety of headlines that were from near-contemporaneous times, and which pointed to some of the common uses of the terms, or labels, "right-wing" and "left-wing." While those headlines are now dated in terms of the calendar, they are just as representative of past usage (over the past approximately 100 years), current usage, and likely future usage (unless the world reads this and understands their foolishness and folly) as they were then. I reprint them below simply to the end of saving time on finding currently dated headlines that represent the exact same sentiment.

Straight from the headlines:

"Bob Dole criticizes Ted Cruz—says he's on extreme right wing," *Townhall*, 4-22-14

"Right wing's surge in Europe has establishment rattled," *New York Times*, 11-8-13

"Right wing militias and the NRA: Second Amendment soulmates," *Huffington Post*, 5-25-11

"Attempted left wing lynching attacks personal integrity," *Reader Supported News*, 10-2-14

"Three failed attempts of right wing media to dismiss the facts of NYT Benghazi Report," *Media Matters*, 11-2-14

"Here's why your favorite horror movies are so left wing," *Daily Beast*, 10-31-14

"Tiny band of left wing radicals bring jobs policy to its knees," *The Telegraph*, 2-25-12

"Obama FBI partners with left wing extremist group," *Townhall*, 11-25-13

Left-wing horror movies? Right-wing media? The references are everywhere and are applied to everything. These phrases are tossed about so frequently and casually in today's America that people using them assume that everyone knows what they are talking about. The people hearing them assume that the people using them must know what they are talking about.

The truth is that nobody knows what anybody is talking about anymore, and that typically includes the person doing the talking. America is coming apart at the seams, and everybody is shouting as loudly as they can at anyone they can find. One of the key drivers of the division in America today is the use of imprecise, pejorative language coupled with a complete misunderstanding of the actual underlying political/sociological structure.

As should be already clear from the Paul-Hitler example cited above, there is no universal agreement as to the meaning of what people are saying when they apply political labels to one another, and to the extent there is agreement, the agreement that is reached has been built upon false premises. As a general rule, whenever you ask someone to define a term or concept that is objective in nature, if they start by saying, "I think it means," then, the truth is, it doesn't really mean anything at all.

This problem can be solved only through education and illumination. I need you to be willing to challenge things you previously thought, or "knew," to be true and consider a fresh way to view issues and engage in constructive debate and dialogue. When you are done reading this, it is my hope that you will never:

a. Use the terms "right-left" when discussing politics.
b. Listen to politicians, pundits, or professors the same way again.
c. Hear a story in the news and consider it the way you did before.
d. Have a disagreement on an issue with someone and not understand how they got to their position.

Conversely, it is my hope that after reading this you will always:

a. Think through your positions and understand if you developed them thoughtfully or reflexively.
b. Be able to solve political policy problems with other people (if you get them to read this, too).
c. Evaluate a proposed piece of legislation or other government action based upon its impact on individual freedom.

I also believe that after you read this, you will be able to easily understand things that might currently seem to be inexplicable. When following current events, have you ever wondered why our government leaders can't:

- Get together to address the immigration problem;
- Set limits on the powers of federal police to surveil citizens;
- Reform a tax code that is so complex and unfair that nobody likes it;
- Come to some reasonable terms on the matter of abortion?

AMERICA IS GOING OUT OF BUSINESS

My professional experience has been comprised of spending over forty years in the business world, many of those years devoted to turning around troubled companies. Whenever I would start a turnaround engagement, it would commence by having all the key members of the organization, sometimes including their outside professionals, assemble in a conference room. Every meeting, while unique, would start in a similar manner with me sitting at the head of the table and saying something like this: "I know everybody in this room is frustrated and worried. You're in a very bad spot. Here's the thing: If we don't walk out of this room with a plan that is realistic and that you can all buy into, then you aren't going to make payroll next week. If that happens, you're out of business."

America has been going out of business for some time. Why then don't leaders and citizens get together to solve problems just like businesspeople do in the non-political world? I'm writing this in part as an attempt to address that question and, as a by-product, perhaps help the country move forward without going out of business.

An aside: Not all troubled companies are able to turn around. The same is true for nations. America needs a successful turnaround, and to make that happen, we need a better understanding of the true causes and effects of our division. Let's get started.

THE INCOHERENCE OF

"TEAM RIGHT" AND "TEAM LEFT"

Keeping in mind that this was originally published in 2015, current events were drawn from in order to provide illustrations. I intend to keep those illustrations throughout because, as mentioned at the outset, their representations of key elements of my arguments remain accurate.

Were I writing this fresh in 2023, I likely would have used the George Floyd incident in Minneapolis (Floyd dying as a result of a confrontation with police) from Memorial Day in 2020 in place of the Ferguson, Missouri example mentioned below. Take note as you read the 2015 text how easily I could have made that substitution. It will help validate my contentions later on. Likewise, you will be able to see how I could have substituted the incident in Charlottesville, Virginia in 2017 (a protestor was killed by another protestor labeled as a white supremacist who ran them down with an automobile) for the Wade Michael Page reference.

On August 9, 2014, Michael Brown, an 18-year-old Black teenager in Ferguson, Missouri was shot and killed by Darren Wilson, an on-duty, 28-year-old white police officer. Brown had just been involved in the robbery of a convenience store, but Wilson was not aware of that fact (he was aware there had been a robbery).

As Wilson was responding to the incident, he encountered Brown and a friend walking down the middle of the street, blocking traffic. After stopping to instruct them to move, he then realized they matched the description of the robbery suspects. What ensued was a confrontation that led to the shooting death of Brown and polarized the nation. He was unarmed at the time. A grand jury investigation concluded that Wilson was justified in the shooting incident, and no charges or disciplinary action would be brought against the officer.

Two years earlier on August 5, 2012, Wade Michael Page, a former military veteran and a member of a white supremacist rock band, walked into a Sikh temple in Oak Creek, Wisconsin and murdered six temple members before taking his own life after he was wounded by police. It is speculated that Page thought he was killing Muslims but didn't study religious geography very well. The error only compounded the senselessness of the tragedy.

What did these two seemingly unrelated criminal events have in common with one another? On their face, they would seem to be stand-alone incidents, each with their own set of facts and preceding series of events that are always fascinating to criminologists. What they weren't, under any reasonable interpretation, were political events.

Or were they?

Immediately after each of these events, media members, political and social commentators, and politicians began making statements. In the Ferguson case, on one side there were people defending the police officer for the shooting, even though the teenager was unarmed. On the other side, political hucksters like Al Sharpton were screaming racism before they even learned Brown had just committed a crime. In the Oak Creek case, because of Page's affiliation with white supremacist groups, and his devotion to William Pierce's 1978 racist novel *The Turner Diaries*, which revolves around the overthrow of the U.S. government, commentators called him a "right-wing extremist." Eager journalists searched unsuccessfully to see if they could find a connection to the Tea Party.

Why would people jump to make a political point out of law enforcement matters? More importantly, why would people automatically, reflexively, come to the defense of one side or the other, or render judgment on what happened, and why before any facts were even known? The answer lies at the heart of the current deep division found in American society, a division that is often called the battle between the "right wing" and the "left wing."

The battle that is better described as "Team Right" vs. "Team Left."

In this sort of paradigm, people talk past each other instead of talking to each other. There is no rational debate on issues and no attempt to work toward an acceptable solution; there is only positioning to win at all costs—to attain complete victory for your side or position or at least hold the other side to a stalemate. In short, when addressing an issue that needs to be addressed, Americans behave more like members of opposing teams who are trying to win a game than as citizens of a civilized, free nation who need to find workable and acceptable solutions to problems.

Teams play to win, to defeat their opponent. Nations need to unify in order to compete against opponents outside of their borders—other nations. This isn't working.

MORE HEADLINE NONSENSE

During the NSA surveillance scandal in 2014, then Fox News commentator Brit Hume was on Bill O'Reilly's program discussing the matter. O'Reilly was pointing out that people on both the far left and the far right were objecting to the NSA. Hume responded by explaining that at their extremes the far right and far left actually touch each other.

Really? Exactly how does that work? People who are diametrically opposed to one another suddenly do complete reversals, all of their profound differences go away, and they agree on everything? Does that mean that fascists and communists become one? Libertarians and progressives? Republicans and Democrats?

Please. That is complete nonsense. It's the kind of thing that people say that sounds very deep and intellectual at first, but when you stop to think about it, you can quickly realize that it is without any foundation or support. "Nonsense" is actually too soft a term. It is an act of aggressive assault upon reason.

You can't draw any kind of political continuum that bends like Beckham, or Einstein, and touches itself at extremes. That would actually make it some form of an ellipse, and there wouldn't, or couldn't, even be any extremes by definition!

Consider these current event examples from 2014–15 when this piece was originally written. It is just as easy, and therefore unnecessary, to find similar examples in 2023 that make the same points. Each of these clearly highlights the inconsistent and utterly meaningless use of the terms right-wing and left-wing.

- Israeli youth kill a Palestinian youth during the violence on the West Bank, and the news characterizes them as "right-wing extremists." Taliban leaders order the execution of women who violate Islamic law, and they are referred to as "far-right clerics." So if we have this right, Israelis and Muslims who have been warring with each other for centuries are both of the same political persuasion and shared ideology.

- Hobby Lobby claims that it should not have to provide contraception to its employees under ObamaCare because it objects to the requirement in principle. The news then reports of "far-left" groups protesting against Hobby Lobby's position. This means that if you think making businesses pay for employees' contraception is the right and necessary thing to do, you're close to being a . . . ??? Communist? Progressive?

- Adam Corolla talks about family values being an issue in minority communities, and he is attacked by "far-left" activist groups for being racist and "too far right." This means that one side likes families and one side doesn't like families but it is difficult to know which is which.

Maybe both sides like and dislike families, and they are touching at the extremes?

There is almost always inconsistent and contradictory use of the terms "left-wing" and "right-wing" when describing events and political positions. In general, however, it seems that people tend to be referring to Republican types when saying right-wing and to Democrat types when saying left-wing.

Maybe the confusion is okay if everyone is getting to the same place anyway?

But what if they aren't?

Why does it matter what terms we use if we all agree about what we are saying? The short answer to that question is that it doesn't unless you're an admirer of precise language. The problem with the use of "right and left" in America today is that we don't all agree on what the terms mean.

Consider the use of the terms "kleenex" or "scotch tape." Notice that the terms are typed as nouns and not as proper nouns (which they should be). It is very common for people to ask for a "kleenex" when they are sneezing or for a piece of "scotch tape" when they are wrapping a present. That's because those terms have commonly become known as representing all tissue and all adhesive strips. When you ask for one or the other, you might not get the right brand, but you will get what you were expecting.

On the other hand, when you use the terms "right wing" and "left wing," they can mean very different things to different people, and what's worse, they might not even mean the same thing consistently to the same person.

Let's take a minute to clarify a couple of terms. First, the terms "right" and "left" indicate direction, and not just direction but opposing direction. When we say someone is "far" right or "far" left, the use of the term "far" necessitates that there is a finite endpoint to what being right and being left mean. You cannot be "far" in any direction on a line of infinite length.

The rational deduction based on the above is that if we say someone is "far right," we should know that they are at the very edge of a very knowable endpoint.

But in the way we use those terms today, that simply isn't the case.

FOUR WRONGS DON'T MAKE A RIGHT

Below is what inspired the slide presentation that I mentioned at the beginning, the one that includes a series of two different persons an audience is asked to categorize. Here is what I used in 2015 to make the original point.

Let's consider four different figures from the past 100 years, each of whom can be easily Googled to find numerous references to them being "far right." First, let's take Benito Mussolini, the father of fascism, who ruled Italy from 1922 to 1945 and was Hitler's ally in World War II.

Next there is Ayn Rand, an early-twentieth-century immigrant to the United States who came from post-revolution Russia. Rand is the mother of the philosophy called "Objectivism," which places reason above all other attributes in terms of importance. She is likewise the author of the novel *Atlas Shrugged*, which laid out the principles of Objectivism through the exploits of the mysterious protagonist John Galt.

Now add Oklahoma City bomber and domestic terrorist Timothy McVeigh to the list along with former U.S. Senator and 2012 Republican presidential primary contender Rick Santorum.

Four "far right" people who, by definition, ought to agree on just about everything, right (perhaps "correct?" would be better)? The problem is they don't.

Benito Mussolini was an atheist who referred to priests as "black germs" but who tolerated the presence of the Catholic Church in Italy. In 1927, he outlawed abortion under his "Battle for Births" program to increase the population. He used gun control policies to disarm his citizenry and make it impossible for them to revolt. He was an early-age admirer of Marx and extolled the benefits of National Socialism. He outlawed labor unions in Italy and wanted every citizen to identify themselves first and foremost as Italians. He sought a strong national identity. Mussolini was responsible for the deaths of innocents to solidify his power and show Italian supremacy not just in Italy, but also in Ethiopia, which he invaded in 1935 and where he used poison gas in an attempt to wipe out the Ethiopian people.

Ayn Rand was an ardent capitalist who despised Mussolini and his socialist policies. She was a supporter of a woman's right to an abortion without restriction, owing to her belief that our true humanity comes from our ability to reason, which certainly an unborn fetus/child cannot yet do. Rand was also an atheist, pro-union (but anti-coercion), anti-gun control, and pro–death penalty (cautiously). Rand believed that government should have little to do with interfering in individual lives and that each person should hold their own self-fulfillment, indeed selfishness, as their primary virtue. Nobody, in her mind, should voluntarily subordinate their personal identity to the State. Rand would never advocate the taking of human life to further a political objective.

Timothy McVeigh was essentially an emotionally disturbed, single-issue citizen who was a strict constructionist of the U.S. Constitution but who mostly was preoccupied by the Second Amendment and the right to keep and bear arms. He is considered a far-right figure in part because he had read *The Turner Diaries*, the same book read by Wade Michael Page. However, McVeigh studied it because of its emphasis on the perils of the government confiscating citizen's firearms. McVeigh actually was *not* a fascist or a Nazi admirer and at one time passed out pamphlets entitled "United States Government or Nazi Germany?"—which compared the excesses of our government to that of Hitler's. He was born Catholic, strayed from his faith, and reportedly did receive sacraments near his execution. McVeigh struggled with racism throughout his life and did not, per se, consider himself to be a white supremacist. He did, however, decide to kill a lot of people to make his voice heard.

Former U.S. Senator Rick Santorum is a devout Catholic with strong pro-life beliefs. He has expressed mixed feelings over the death penalty. His legislative record was one showing a mixed voting record on labor union issues and a clear record on supporting "pork barrel" programs that brought government tax dollars back to Pennsylvania. Ayn Rand would find his votes on economic matters contemptuous. He is a strong gun-rights advocate who believes the Second Amendment exists to protect the First Amendment. While he can certainly be called a "crony capitalist," he would just as certainly decry the economic policies of Mussolini's fascist Italy. He also would abhor the taking of innocent human life for any reason.

Based on the above, you can clearly see that these four "far right" people, if placed into a locked room with one another, would last about five minutes before going after one another like cats trapped in a laundry bag. But how can that be? They are all "far right," which means they all must see close to eye-to-eye?

Maybe the terms don't mean what people think they mean? Maybe they don't really mean anything at all?

How could we possibly have gotten to the point where so many people use the same terms to describe completely different types of beliefs and behaviors?

THE EXACT PROBLEM
WE FACE WITH RIGHT-LEFT LABELS

Having identified the absolute nonsense of the right-left labels by pointing to the intellectually indefensible use of the terms, we now must replace what is described with what actually is; we must define the terms. Before doing that, however, let's address what is at the heart of the problem when it comes to understanding the differences between Americans politically.

The key problem is this: We keep trying to describe where people are in their political beliefs by using something directional (right-left), which is a horizontal and continuous structure. Instead, we should be using a vertical and stratified model to describe their political beliefs and a horizontal model only to show the level of intensity with which they are willing to impose them upon others. One model doesn't cut it. You have to have two, and fortunately, I will provide them shortly.

Allow me to use a friend of mine as an example of the problem, not because I believe she is representative of the general population in her views, but because her views are representative of the problem we have when using right-left labels in trying to characterize someone's politics.

My friend is an extreme sort of believer in a free market economic structure, but not because she necessarily thinks it is virtuous. She believes in it because she thinks it is the only way to channel human nature in its least destructive manner. She is a deist who believes that while the Judeo-Christian ideals that run through the veins of Western Civilization played a significant role in our nation's founding, no religious beliefs should play any part in policy making or governance. She is against the death penalty and for a woman's right to choose through the early stages of pregnancy up to a certain point where she feels believes abortion transitions into infanticide.

She is in favor of same-sex marriage but thinks that the decision to marry in today's America is an irrational mistake.

To continue, she believes that the United States should largely abstain from any military involvement in foreign wars and should do so only when its national security interest is directly threatened. When it is necessary to use our military, she believes in using it with whatever sort of ruthlessness is needed to ensure swift and complete victory. She thinks the United Nations should be abolished and the World Economic Forum should be ignored. Large corporations and the people who run them are generally corrupt and dangerous at their core, and Wall Street types routinely and joyously seek to exploit the American working man and woman.

She is strongly against a federal police force, strongly against government regulation of the internet, and generally favors the legalization of drugs (despite personally being in recovery).

Now, using the above information, I ask you, is my friend right- or left-wing? My follow-up question is: Having identified her as either right or left, how far right or far left is she? Finally, now defend your answer to yourself and see how many knots you're tied into by the time you are done.

I think, if you are being honest, you will have to acknowledge that there is no way to take the information I just shared with you and place the sum total of those views on some sort of right-left line. The current right-left paradigm attempts to take a very complex, multi-variable condition and make it binary.

Now I am going to give you one final personal data point about my friend that you can take along through the rest of this chapter. It is: She is fundamentally opposed to the use of government, especially the federal government, to turn into a law every good idea that might exist, including her own good ideas.

What I am hoping to illustrate is that our opinions about particular issues exist independently of our willingness to use the government to impose them upon others. Our opinions on issues *can* impact our willingness to use government, but they do not do so necessarily.

What I failed to share with you when disclosing some of my friend's personal positions is the level of intensity she feels about each of them. It isn't important that I do so for this exercise, but it is vitally important that you keep in mind the concept of intensity and bring it along as you continue reading. I will point out later why the intensity of different policy opinions matters to an individual and how it impacts their political affiliations and behavior.

Remember to be thinking about the differences between horizontal and continuous versus vertical, discrete, and hierarchical.

ORIGINS OF A
DIVIDED AMERICAN SPECIES

Under the Microscope: The Political Continuum?

As we've discussed, the use of terms "right" and "left" establishes that there is directionality, and the use of the term "far" means there are endpoints. Put all this together and you're left with the implication that you're moving along a line—a continuum. In this case, a political continuum.

The origins of our current political continuum are explained below. For now, let's simply define what it is in its most common form.

L	X	M	Y	R
Communist		Moderate		Fascist

Figure 2.

The model shown in Figure 2 has communism at the far left and fascism at the far right. A moderate is found at the midpoint.

Variations and deviations from this model have been formulated for the past fifty years. They have taken many shapes and forms, some even being represented as a quadrant diagram or a 3D rendering. These elaborate models look more like a personality profile than anything having to do with political thought movement, but that's indicative of the struggle to clearly show the dichotomies and progressions of political positions.

While there are numerous problems with this continuum, perhaps the most obvious is that of characterizing points X and Y marked above. Who are those people? What do they, and what don't they, believe in? The difficulty in answering these questions was alluded to earlier when I shared the viewpoints of my friend. The problem with this political continuum and the representation of right and left is that it attempts to depict a continuous data pattern in a directional path that doesn't exist. Additionally, it is trying to attach the role of government power to that of viewpoints on issues. The idea that you can equate type of government to positions on issues is a complete non sequitur and yet we have been mixing the two for generations.

Everything comes from something, so I want to take time to trace the origins. After that, I will show how America has taken the left-right fallacy and perverted it into what I describe as Team Left and Team Right. By the end of this process, how we have come to destroy both language and logic in our political conversations will become crystal clear.

It is easy to hear the casual terms "right and left" and assume that they have been around since the beginning of man and have always held the same universal meaning. That's never the case with language, and it is especially not the case here. As we have already shown, as the terms are currently used, they have no universally agreed-upon meaning. How we got to this point explains a lot of this ambiguity. More importantly, understanding how we got here provides insight into how to change the way we use language, define terms, and have discussions. It provides light along the path to healing.

We need to discard the current dysfunctional paradigm and replace it with one that can predict patterns and show opportunities for coming together and solving problems.

There are clear historical events and developments that have brought us to where we are at this moment in time. Let's take a look at each of them, in order, and see if it doesn't help explain just about everything with regard to how we use terms and categorize people today.

This journey is a sort of evolution, the first part of which forms the commonly accepted paradigm of today (right wing–left wing) with the second part showing how Americans have sort of adapted their individual and group behaviors in an attempt to conform to the paradigm. Unfortunately, because of the deficiency in the paradigm's formation, it is unable to sustain political life.

We begin our journey in France.

THE FRENCH REVOLUTION: THE BIRTH OF "RIGHT WING" AND "LEFT WING"

The Assemblée Nationale (National Assembly) was convened in June 1789 in pre-revolutionary France. It was led by the Third Estate (the commoners or "people"), who then offered participation to the members of the First Estate (the clergy in its entirety) and the Second Estate (French nobility, excluding the monarch, who was outside the "Estate" system). These were the very people in support of King Louis XVI (the monarch), the man and institution the Revolution would ultimately overthrow. The Third Estate had the members of the First and the Second sit on the right side of the chamber because in French culture it was considered proper etiquette to have your guests sit to the right of the host (as most people are right-handed).

As a result of the seating arrangement, the people sitting on the right side were the supporters of the French monarchy (right wing), and the people sitting on the left side were the commoners supporting what can be loosely called democracy (left wing). It is this time and place where the terms "right wing" and "left wing" originated. While the French Revolution went on to become notoriously violent, temporarily victorious, and ultimately wiped away by Napoleon, the terms "right wing" and "left wing" would survive.

It's important to note that there was no political continuum yet that had a left and a right endpoint. There were just two sides; the monarchists on the right and the social democrats on the left.

In short, the terms that divide America today and have us talking past each other instead of to each other came about because of French table manners and furniture arrangements.

THE RUSSIAN REVOLUTION: LENIN CO-OPTS THE "LEFT"

Everyone knows about the Bolshevik Revolution and the beginnings of "Communist" Russia in 1917. What isn't as widely known is the impact that Revolution would have on how Americans would ultimately come to describe themselves politically.

Vladimir Lenin was an admirer of the instigators of the French Revolution. He admired their spirit, studied their ability to foment a mob, and learned from their failures in terms of not being able to solidify and hold power on a long-term basis. He spoke and wrote about the French Revolution, extolling its virtues and warning against its failures. Lenin positioned his revolution as that of the workers: the common people uniting against the Czar (the monarchy). The world took notice of the similarities to the French experience and came to see the Russian Revolution as essentially the second French Revolution. One offshoot of that was the newly minted term "communist," a contemporary and intellectually trendy fit for the "left wing" heading, created almost a century and a half earlier in France. In the early twentieth century, "communism" now took a seat in the left wing of casual political language.

MUSSOLINI, HITLER, FASCISM, NAZISM, AND CHOOSING SIDES IN WORLD WAR II

Europe was a dangerous and rapidly changing place after the end of World War I. Mussolini brought fascism to Italy, making the trains run on time and making his opponents just run. Lenin and then Stalin consolidated what was being called "communism" inside Russia and neighboring countries like Ukraine; Stalin systematically starved to death up to 11 million people. Franco brought totalitarianism to Spain in 1939 with the help of Mussolini and the increasingly powerful corporal from Germany: Adolph Hitler.

On the other side of the world, Imperial Japan was dusting off samurai swords and fueling "zeros."

The United States watched carefully and nervously as events unfolded across two oceans, hoping to stay out of the war raging around them. December 7, 1941 made that hope disappear. Once America was attacked by Japan, a member of the Axis Powers along with Italy and Germany, there was no keeping it out of the world conflict.

Despite official problems with the communist government of Russia, the United States now found itself an uncomfortable ally with the murderer Stalin in taking on the Axis. While it is difficult to argue about the choice we made to throw in with the Soviets, there was an unintended consequence that has had a lasting impact on American domestic politics to this day.

Hitler and Stalin were the same type of guy. They were bloodthirsty, totalitarian monsters who sought power through conquest and had no reservations about murdering anyone necessary in order to attain and retain it. Their economic systems and political structures differed in specifics but were essentially the same in results: They controlled everything, and their people lived in fear and slavery.

In order to side with one bad guy against the other, we the world needed to make them different. Politically, that meant placing Nazism and fascism as the polar opposite of communism. Remember, communism had already claimed the "left-wing" position before the war. Now, at last, the dated concept of "monarchists" could be replaced with something more contemporary seated in the "right wing." Fascism and Nazism would hereafter lay claim to the "right."

I pause at this point to make clear that the abovementioned events are what gave us the terms "left wing" and "right wing" and their generally accepted end-point references (communism-fascism). The supposed continuum is a horizontal line showing continuous movement. Further, it more accurately represents different types of governing models. Distilling those into a linear model is demonstrably wrong and plainly absurd. Although people have been recklessly using the right-left terms to describe political positions, this is inaccurate and even destructive to at best clear communication, at worst genuine collaboration and problem-solving.

We just established that, by the end of World War II, we had settled upon the accepted continuum. That continuum provided a sort of preformed paradigm in which two opposing American political teams began to be formed. Some of the differing team elements (or "platoons," as I will call them),such as the "Labor Movement," actually formed prior to World War II, but they didn't have any sort of structure to slip into.

What I will now illustrate is how America took the notion of right-left directional opposition, the labels we created for those at the extremes, and built an entire political "team vs. team" operational structure that today accounts for all of our division and constant infighting as a nation.

One final note before continuing: Although there have been numerous sorts of political continuums and categories created over time, all of which are defective, the continuum identified and described above is the one that has given us the foundation of our current right-left terminology. No other model influences the right-left labeling in any manner. Just as all philosophers for over two thousand years have been answering Plato, all other political models have been answering the fascism-communism model. Like Plato, this model continues to haunt us.

POST WORLD WAR II
"HUNTS FOR COMMUNISTS"
–U.S. TEAMS START TO FORM

After the War and seemingly in an effort to cleanse its palate of the aftertaste of cozying up to the Soviets, American political leaders turned their attention towards looking for communists right here in the United States. They went looking in two general categories: political/public servants and/or citizens in positions of influence within the general population. Chief amongst the latter category were members of the Hollywood film industry.

While the era and events in question have come under the general historical heading "McCarthyism," the truth is that Wisconsin Senator Joe McCarthy sat on a committee that primarily looked for communists inside the Truman Administration, especially the State Department. It was the House Un-American Activities Committee (HUAC) that went after Hollywood. HUAC was established in 1938 and lasted until 1975. Despite its long run, its truly impactful years were those immediately following World War II.

An examination of HUAC membership during the committee's existence, and from the mid-'40s to the mid-'50s, shows back-and-forth control between Republicans and Democrats. This was a bipartisan affair. That said, the Republicans were seen as being more zealous in their pursuit of communists while the Democrats were more "reserved" in their approach. Democrats did not want to appear too extreme in either direction with regard to the matter because of the following slightly confusing reasoning:

- Democrats did not want to appear to support communists and, by extension, the Soviet Union.
- The Russian Revolution had ostensibly been a workers' revolution.
- Organized labor generally favored the preferences preached (not practiced) by communist party members.
- Democrats were political partners with organized labor.

So the Republicans were seen as being "more" anti-communist in part for real reasons and in part because Republican Joe McCarthy was the poster child for what the press called a "witch hunt."

When HUAC went after the group that came to be known as the "Hollywood Ten," writers and producers who were called to testify in October 1947, the nation in general, and Hollywood in particular, took notice. These people were all suspected of being members of, or associating with, the Communist Party. In their testimony they were asked to affirm or deny, for the record, their affiliation with communists and they were also asked to name names of other Hollywood members they knew or believed to be communists. They refused to cooperate. All ten were cited for contempt, sent to prison, and blacklisted from working in Hollywood when they were let out.

This period in American history had two very significant impacts on the formation of "Team Right" and "Team Left." The first was in Hollywood, where, once it had licked its wounds and stopped trembling from the HUAC hearings, the film industry (ultimately spreading to entertainment in general) would assert itself against the "right wing" and would strongly stand against the side that persecuted it.

This would come to be reflected in both the attitudes of its stars and the ideas expressed in its films (compare the kind of movies Hollywood made about America before 1950 to those it made after 1960; there was a transitional decade). The other impact it had was to label Republicans as anti-communist and, therefore, "right-wing." The formulation goes like this:

- Republicans presented themselves as strong anti-communists.
- We just fought with the communists against the fascists/Nazis.
- Communists are left-wing.
- Republicans are right-wing, the opposite of communists, and now are to be associated with fascists/Nazis in terms of their points of view[2].

There was another team-building and divisive development that came out of the "McCarthy Era." The House and Senate investigations hit their height in the early 1950s during the dawn of television and television journalism. Then CBS News reporter, and now-industry icon, Edward R. Murrow ruled the airwaves as the original investigative television journalist. Murrow had become famous as a war correspondent for CBS, where he covered the Nazi invasion of Austria, the bombing of London, and other major World War II events. After the war, Murrow eventually started an investigative TV show

---

2   . . . and since Democrats were on the softer side of the hearings in general, they became associated as being more friendly to communists and, therefore, "left-wing."

called *See It Now*. It was on that show that he relentlessly attacked Joe McCarthy, ultimately leading to McCarthy making an appearance on the show to explain and defend himself. It did not go well. McCarthy ultimately disappeared in shame, and Murrow would go down in journalistic history as the man who slayed the witch hunter.

Murrow's ascendancy to the pinnacle of the investigative journalist platform has led him to be revered both directly and indirectly for the last three generations of journalists. There is an almost biblical lineage that can be traced (Murrow begat Cronkite; Cronkite begat Rather and Brokaw; Brokaw begat Williams, then Holt, etc.). These big celebrity names and faces of journalism are representative of the lesser-known, but Murrow-inspired, core of the Fourth Estate (a term applied to the press with its origins tracing back to eighteenth-century England), which today finds itself largely in support of Team Left, their cheerleading position established by Edward R. Murrow over a half century ago.

THE CIVIL RIGHTS MOVEMENT AND CIVIL RIGHTS ACT–NEW TEAM MEMBERS RECRUITED

The Civil Rights Movement that started in the 1950s segregated the South and culminated with President Kennedy's proposal of the Civil Rights Act (CRA) in 1963, which became law after his death in 1964. Ironically enough, President Kennedy had been slow to embrace civil rights legislation and required a great deal of persuading from his brother, Attorney General Robert Kennedy. Perhaps it is less ironic when you consider that the South was largely governed by Democrats. That's right. The party that today is associated with protecting minority interests was, in very recent history, the party in charge of suppressing those interests.

So how could it possibly become the case that Blacks would come to join "Team Left" and become such captured members of the very party who had suppressed them for decades? The answer is complex but clear and has impacted American politics now for over fifty years.

After the assassination of Kennedy, Democrats and Republicans alike sought to honor his memory by passing the bill which Kennedy had supported. That said, the Southern Democrats did not support the

Act, and that is reflected in the final vote tallies, which show them voting overwhelmingly against it. However, there were enough Democrats in the North to combine with strong Republican support to get the legislation through. That's right, the Republican Party House and Senate members were far more receptive to the CRA.

Immediately after the CRA became law, the next string of legislation related to Lyndon Johnson's "Great Society" programs. This was the beginning of the modern-day welfare state. Johnson had received enormous support in the wake of Kennedy's assassination and when the 89th Congress was elected in 1964, Democrats outnumbered Republicans by a margin of 68–32 in the Senate and 295–140 in the House. Lyndon Johnson and the Democrats could do whatever they wanted to do. What they did with that power was create a whole series of entitlement programs that would make large groups of people dependent upon the government not just for assistance, but for subsistence.

Of course, one of the lowest income groups around was Blacks, who had been kept down on, and often kept off, the economic ladder. Democrats immediately saw them as potential consumers of welfare state benefits and artfully developed them as a constituency. Democrats came to be seen as the party of the poor; the struggling; the oppressed (forget that just minutes earlier they had been the oppressors). With Republicans generally opposed to expansive welfare programs, they became seen as threats to the minority community.

But there was more to it than just a disagreement on policy and economics.

Remember that just a decade before Republicans had been determined to be "right-wingers," the ones who opposed communism. Remember, too, that World War II had led us to define the opposite of communists to be fascists, or Nazis. Fresh in the memory of every American was our recent clash with the most notorious racist of modern history and the poster child for "right-wingers. . ."

THE CORPORAL TURNED
FÜHRER IN GERMANY

So began the portrayal of Republicans, the right-wingers, being opposed to welfare programs and helping minorities because they were inherently racist. After all, that's what it meant to be a "far right" person and what could be more "far right" than saying you didn't want to feed poor Black children living in Mississippi?

From that point on, it got easy. Not only did Team Left attract and hold Blacks, but other minority groups began to join Team Left. These groups often felt, and still feel (sometimes rightly), they've been victimized or not given a fair shake and they need a helping hand in the form of government assistance.

Today, it is nearly considered dogma that Team Left is the one that takes care of minorities and their interests and Team Right is constantly fighting its inherent racist tendencies; at best ignoring those minorities and, at worst, attempting to enact policy that will be deliberately detrimental to their interests.

Sadly, for Team Right, while the remaining racists are a very small minority in this country, since having seen the minorities move en masse to Team Left, many of them decided that the only place they could be was Team Right. There aren't as many of them around anymore, but any time Team Left finds one hiding on the Team Right sideline, they point a bright shining light on them and say, "See. I told you they were there."

Finally, when a minority group leader shows overt signs of reverse racism, they are seldom seriously criticized; certainly not by their teammates. After all, they have been loyal team members for over fifty years, and isn't that the reason that they joined the team in the first place? That they were victims of racism; racism from right-wingers?

If this seems confusing, wait until you see what the Vietnam War did to team membership.

VIETNAM – TEAM RIGHT AND TEAM LEFT
PICK UP (LAY DOWN) THEIR WEAPONS

It is easy to make the argument that the Vietnam War was the most significant event in American military history. That argument gets made not because of the outcome of the war (other wars, Revolutionary, Civil, World War II, would be more important in that regard), but because of the seemingly permanent effect it had on both dividing the country and governing how America would, and would not, wage war thereafter. The nation's wounds from Vietnam are still raw, open, and painful today.

Regardless of a person's opinion about the use of military power in general, or its use in Vietnam in particular, it is impossible to argue that the war itself was not a colossal example of mismanagement on the part of U.S. leadership. Our involvement started in the early 1960s under the Kennedy Administration and escalated under Lyndon Johnson, the war, which ultimately claimed over 58,000 U.S. casualties, was fought as a containment conflict against an enemy that was striving for all-out victory. It was destined for failure before it ever started.

It was in 1961 that President Kennedy began sending in military advisors and not until January 27, 1973 when the Paris Peace Accords were signed that the fighting ended. The twelve-year duration of the war made it the longest U.S. military engagement up until that time. America left after these twelve years having essentially helped the South Vietnamese battle with the North Vietnamese culminate in a draw. Two years after the U.S. withdrawal, Saigon would fall to the North Vietnamese and America's waste of blood and treasure was complete.

Vietnam was the first war that saw the use of television to bring the battlefield into every American's living room on a nightly basis. The graphic images of American casualties, combined with the long duration of the war and the seeming lack of progress toward victory, led to anger on the part of many Americans. A significant portion of America, especially the youth who were being involuntarily drafted to go to Southeast Asia to fight, were becoming anti-war, anti-military, and anti-U.S. in general.

Consider the change in American attitudes brought about by Vietnam. When our involvement started in earnest in 1961, we were only sixteen years removed from having been victorious in one of history's most significant confrontations: World War II. Americans might have been war weary after that victory but they were anything but anti-military (there were isolationists leading up to, and even during World War II, but that was a different kind of position than the one born during Vietnam). It took a protracted and bungled use of American wealth and excessive loss of American lives to split the nation on the matter of using American military power to create an impact overseas.

So how did the Vietnam War impact American right-wing and left-wing politics? It is very interesting to note that the war was started and escalated by two Democratic presidents (Kennedy and Johnson). This might seem ironic, or at least inconsistent, until you remember the slow evolution of America into teams. During the McCarthy Era, Democrats were not "pro-communist" per se. They were simply softer on the issue. Kennedy and Johnson were both Democrats who were concerned about the Soviet Union and its spreading of their form of government to other regions of the world. They saw Vietnam as a communist beachhead in the region that had to be contained, if not rolled back.

Let's get basic. Who were we fighting in Vietnam? The North Vietnamese communists, of course. And on which side of the political continuum were communists? Left. And anti-communists? Right. The movement that was forming against the war had to not just find a political home somewhere, it needed to build one. The logical place for them to break ground and homestead was the Democratic Party, which had already shown its Team Left tendencies. So, the anti-war, anti-military, often anti-U.S. crowd began its takeover attempt of the Democratic Party in 1968 with riots outside of the DNC convention site in Chicago and completed that takeover with the nomination of George McGovern as the party's presidential candidate in 1972. From that point forward, the Democratic Party and Team Left would contain the anti-military "platoon," a term I'll discuss more below.

Of course, many Americans who still believed in the rightness of American action wherever and whatever it might be were appalled to see the demonstrations against the war and the vocal protestations of people criticizing American soldiers. Those people supported our nation's efforts to ensure the sovereignty of the South Vietnamese and contain the "red menace" of communism. For these Americans, watching the anti-war crowd take over the Democratic Party left them no place to go but to the Republican Party to oppose them. From this split, you could watch the news right up through the mid-2010s and see party members and Team Right–Team Left commentators take almost reflexive positions when discussing any issue involving U.S. foreign intervention and especially use of military power.

That calculation has changed a bit over the past several years and has had an unsettling (generally a good thing) impact on team structure. That will be explained when we get to how the teams are composed.

Vietnam also fortified the membership support of the mainstream American media for Team Left. With the media on the ground in Vietnam for 12-plus years watching the self-inflicted failure of U.S. policy, and with it the death of American troops, reporters there and back at home came to be very anti-war. No single figure represented that shift more than the American legend, and tragically flawed, Walter Cronkite. For years considered the "most trusted man in America," Cronkite anchored the *CBS Evening News* throughout the war and used his calming voice and dignified look to almost single-handedly turn Americans against the effort. His deliberate misreporting of the 1968 Tet Offensive by the North Vietnamese (a victory for U.S. forces that Cronkite characterized as a significant setback, even lying about the occupation of the U.S. Embassy) may have been the single most significant event hastening the ultimate withdrawal of U.S. forces.

With Watergate on the horizon and a Republican the villain, the Fourth Estate was on its way to permanent Team Left cheerleading status.

ROE V. WADE

TRANSLATES INTO RIGHT V. LEFT

There is perhaps no single event in the last 100 years to divide America more than the 1973 Burger Court's decision on abortion (and now its subsequent reversal in 2022 with *Dobbs v. Jackson Women's Health Organization*.) In writing his majority opinion, Justice Harry Blackmun ruled that the Due Process Clause of the Fourteenth Amendment protected a woman's right to privacy and, as follows, her right to an abortion. This took a very controversial issue that had been a matter of individual state legislation for nearly 200 years and gave it blanket sanction under the Constitution.

It seems that both sides in the abortion debate like to cite U.S. history prior to Roe as an argument to support their case. Obviously both sides can't be right, or can they?

I spend more word count here on abortion than on any other issue because in my interviews with people during the composition of this piece, I have found that it might well be the single most determinant issue as to what political team an individual lands upon. The true history of abortion and the laws governing the activity in America are very complicated. It is important to consider that over a 200-year time span, various factors have either changed or evolved. They include:

- The knowledge of when human life begins.
- The capability to save an unborn child.
- The methods available to safely perform an abortion.
- Moral views on the matter, both secular and religious.

The first actual state law prohibiting abortion was passed in 1821 in Connecticut. It involved proscribing the use of poison administered to expectant mothers to induce abortion. From that point forward, states became increasingly inclined to pass laws to either prohibit or restrict abortion (then still a very dangerous medical procedure to the mother. In fact, many of the regulations passed restricting abortion were to actually protect the mother and not the fetus/child), leading up to the passage at the federal level of the Comstock Act in 1873, which banned the dissemination of information about either abortion or birth control.

Anti-abortion attitudes were the prevailing position among U.S. citizens up through 1967 when, at the pro-life zenith, forty-nine States plus the District of Columbia had either severely limited or outright banned abortion. Then the momentum began to shift.

In 1970, first Hawaii and then New York passed laws making abortion legal in the early stages of pregnancy. The Comstock Act started to be repealed in 1971, and prior to the *Roe* case (originating out of Texas), fourteen states had legalized abortion in some form. Clearly the tide was turning.

With *Roe*, the very imperfect and cumbersome process of state-by-state legalizations and restrictions was suddenly and surreptitiously replaced with a one-size-fits-all ruling. Was that a problem? Didn't the United States do just fine with universal recognition of free speech? The right to a fair trial? The elimination of slavery? Unfortunately, regardless of your opinion (really *because* of your opinion), abortion was different.

To those who consider themselves to be "pro-life," abortion is tantamount to murder. They hold to the position that life begins at conception and the taking of that life at any stage is no different than taking the life of a twenty-two-year-old.

For those calling themselves "pro-choice," they see the right of a woman to control what happens inside her own body as being intrinsic to her own humanity and something that should not be dictated to her by others. Some believe human life begins at birth and some concede that life has already begun inside of the woman. Regardless, they see the woman's right to decide for herself about her own health as superseding all other considerations.

So one side thinks it is murder and the other side sees it as an elective medical procedure. This is never going to end well.

When the Supreme Court took the decision out of the hands of the states, it removed the opportunity to craft fifty imperfect, but geographically confined, solutions and replaced that system with one winner and one loser. People could no longer "venue shop" to find the medical and moral climate to suit their liking. Now they were two distinct groups forced to fight on a national level.

Pro-choice members who had long felt oppressed by pro-life members took that natural "civil-rights-challenged" position and joined Team Left. Pro-life people came to Team Right so as to oppose the pro-choice group in full force. Since *Roe*, abortion has been a major issue (explicitly or implicitly) in every election held in the United States. Candidates who run for office, even at levels or positions that will not permit them to act on any abortion matters, are still asked about their positions on the issue. People may well decide to oppose someone based upon their abortion position even if it doesn't relate to the job they'll be doing once in office. More than any other issue, abortion not only drives how a person might vote, it decides how they vote when the issue isn't even involved!

The *Dobbs* decision in 2022 has done nothing to solve the problem between opponents, but it also didn't make it worse. That's a misperception and can easily be explained by the team structure about to be revealed. The *Dobbs* decision didn't heighten differences; it simply elevated the importance of the issue on both teams, which feels like an increase in intensity, especially within their respective platoons.

Consider this. Did the decision in *Dobbs* suddenly make pro-choice or pro-life people become more of what they already were? Of course not. That said, the matter had been a sort of settled law for fifty years with one side holding on and the other side fighting against. The *Dobbs* decision reversed those roles overnight. Imagine an only partially acceptable analogy of firefighters sitting in the station playing cards waiting for an alarm to sound. Now, the two sides on the abortion issue have not just been playing cards for fifty years, but the status quo has also not been materially disrupted. Suddenly overnight, the alarm rang, and it was a five-alarm call. Everybody got up and mobilized. Firefighters at rest are still firefighters; they just aren't in the field containing a blaze.

To stay with the analogy a paragraph longer (because it will be useful to keep in mind for general team dynamics later), when firefighters do have to take to the field, all other community service members clear the way for them and do what is needed to make sure they can do their job. Keep that in mind when we get to the political team hierarchy and shifts within that hierarchy.

A SERIES OF UNFORTUNATE EVENTS HELPS BOTH TEAMS COMPLETE THEIR ROSTERS

In addition to the seismic-movement-type events noted in the preceding sections, there have been other events over the past nine decades that have helped build and solidify Team Right and Team Left. While reasonable people can differ over the inclusion or the exclusion of an event, or its relative importance, here are some that meet the criteria of being identifiable, polarizing, and having lasting and long half-lives within our social/political structure.

THE AMERICAN ORGANIZED LABOR MOVEMENT (1930s)

Before World War II gave us the new political continuum, American labor was a platoon waiting for a team to arrive. The Industrial Revolution gave rise to a working class of blue collar and pink collar workers. Their efforts to form strong unions and stand successfully against their employers were largely unsuccessful. With the election of Franklin Roosevelt to the presidency in 1932, organized labor found its champion. Roosevelt's siding with labor on all fronts—legislation, enforcement, and policy—created an entire class of people who would give birth to "Nth Generation Democrats (see below). They would have to wait for others, but labor became founding members of Team Left.

THE PURSUIT OF THE EQUAL RIGHTS AMENDMENT FOR WOMEN (1970s)

The ERA was pushed aggressively by feminist groups in the late '60s and early '70s. The ERA was an attempt to amend the Constitution to provide women with "equality." The Amendment was passed by the U.S. House and Senate and went to the states for ratification. After a rapid start (getting thirty of the thirty-eight state votes needed), the ERA stalled. The national battle was fierce. Since women who supported the ERA had approached the issue by identifying themselves as oppressed minority victims, their position fit in with the rapidly coming together Team Left. Since then, a majority of women, and a strong majority of feminist women, have been Team Left members.

WATERGATE (EARLY 1970s)

When Richard Nixon's reelection team broke into the Democratic National Campaign Headquarters leading to cover-up, scandal, impeachment, and Nixon's ultimate resignation, the nation was hotly divided. What Watergate did was lead to an overall level of cynicism and distrust of each team by the other. The impact it had on the nation is evidenced today every single time there is a scandal and it is referred to as "Fill-in-the-blank"-gate by the press.

THE CLINTON-LEWINSKY SEX SCANDAL (MID-1990s)

The perceived promiscuity of President Clinton while in office and the news that came from the investigation (like the "Bimbo Patrol" the Clinton campaign had during the 1992 campaign to handle surfacing mistresses) inspired what is called the "religious right." The religious right includes Team Right members with strong Christian beliefs, everything they need to curse the immorality of Team Left. Team Left dug in and defended team member and leader Clinton (the activist and propaganda group MoveOn.org was founded out of the Clinton-Lewinsky scandal). The division remains fresh and frequently referenced to this day.

BUSH V. GORE – THE 2000 PRESIDENTIAL ELECTION

Having lost the popular vote but with the votes of the State of Florida in question, George W. Bush's team of attorneys took the matter to the U.S. Supreme Court, where they ruled in Bush's favor and Florida's electoral votes became enough to put him over the top and into the presidency. Team Left members felt as though the presidency had just been stolen from them. The hatred generated by the contested election was intense and lasting.

THE SECOND IRAQ WAR – NO WEAPONS OF MASS DESTRUCTION (EARLY 2000s)

When President Bush led the United States into war in Iraq as the smoke was still clearing from the 9/11 attacks, he did so by telling the world (and the world agreed) that Saddam Hussein possessed weapons of mass destruction. When no such weapons were produced, the anti-war platoon that had helped form Team Left during Vietnam woke up. After thirty years of lethargy, the anti-war platoon was energized and on the streets. This, in turn, woke up the "hawks" on Team Right, who came to the defense of Bush's policy and the Iraq war almost reflexively. These two groups remain quite active and engaged in battling each other on U.S. soil right up to the minute.

THE BATTLE OVER OBAMACARE

The fight over the federal government taking command and control over one-sixth of the nation's economy energized the members on Team Right and Team Left that see economics as their primary issue (the importance of primary issues is developed more below). Free market advocates see the government intrusion as one that causes disruptions in the supply and demand factors found in medical commerce and will therefore lead to shortages, waste, and aberrant pricing. Socialist economic thinkers see it as a step in the right direction to provide equality in access and service to all citizens regardless of their income levels. Virtually all economic discussions now involve the pejorative use of "capitalist" and "socialist" by both teams regardless of the exact subject of conversation.

THE FIGHT FOR SAME-SEX MARRIAGE AND OTHER LGBTQ ISSUES

The past several years has found increasing efforts both from community members and from outside supporters to expand rights and protections for the LGBTQ people. These efforts have evoked the outrage and indignation of the traditional religious platoon of Team Right. As a result of that hostility, members of the LGBTQ community have found themselves becoming members of Team Left. Even if they might tend to agree with Team Right members on other issues, say, free market economics, they can't be made to feel comfortable with that team because of their primary issue and the resentment they face from certain Team Right members.

THE DIVISIVE PRESIDENCIES OF BARACK OBAMA AND DONALD TRUMP

This is not intended to be a commentary on the positions or the behaviors of either of these two presidents. What is important with regard to the team structure and division in American politics is that both of them were very polarizing figures. Their time in office heightened the resolve and increased the unity of the two teams. While Trump gets routinely mentioned as being this sort of villain of divisiveness, that is because of the power structure that supports the most extreme and boisterous of the Team Left platoons. This will be made clearer in a separate essay later in this book. It is easy to forget the extremely negative reactions Barack Obama's demeanor and policies generated in many Team Right members. Neither really created much in team shifts, but both added to a heightened esprit de corps among the opposition.

THE COVID-19 PANDEMIC AND MEDICAL FREEDOM

The pandemic created an entirely new set of opponents to line up against each other on each team. Not only did it create those new distinctions, it actually caused many team members to either join the other team as free agents, or get them "cut" from their team's roster for violating team rules. I will write more about this development below.

I trust that what I've laid out above makes sound historical sense when you couple the noted events with the general changes that took place within society. Reasonable people can differ as to the severity of any one or more events and can even make the case for an event's inclusion or exclusion. I welcome such discussion and dissent because it means that you are working within the general construct. While there might be disagreement over the degree of impact, it is axiomatic that we got to where we are today through a series of cause-effect occurrences. What I have shared above is my own list of major factors based upon my study and understanding of our history.

Next I want to take a look at who is on what team and what can be done to break apart the team structure completely and get Americans thinking and talking again.

TEAM RIGHT AND TEAM LEFT "PLATOONS"–THE AMERICAN POLITICAL OPERATING MODEL

I have shared my observations as to what have been the major and to some extent lesser but significant events that led to Team Right and Team Left formation. With that as a foundation, the organization of team membership today is shown in Figure 3.

★ ★ ★ ★ ★

American Political Teams

Team Left

Team Right

Team Left	Team Right
• "Nth Generation Democrats"	• "Nth Generation Republicans"
• Pro-Choice	• Pro-Life
• "Green Groups" & Climate Change Activists	• Oil & Gas Supporters
• Gun Control Advocates	• Second Amendment Supporters
• Animal Rights Advocates	• Hunters
• Feminists/LGBTQIA+	• Evangelicals/Fundamentalist Christians
• Racial Preferences	• Strict Libertarians
• Anti-Military	• Pro-Military
• Criminal Justice Reformers	• Strong Law & Order Supporters
• Anti-Capital Pubishment	• Pro-Capital Punishment
• Economic "Socialists"	• Free Market Thinkers
• Unions	• Small Business Owners
• Open Borders	• Strict Immigration Controls
• Pro-Palestinian	• Pro-Israel
• Globalists	• "America First" Nationalists
• Pro-COVID Mandates	• Medical Freedom Movement

*Refers to people who have always considered themselves to be Republicans or Democrats, most often inheriting their party affiliation from long-standing tradition within their families, cultural/community influences, religion, etc. They are what they are simply because those around them are what they are.

**Typically, very strict libertarians who have grown from a variety of philosophers including John Stuart Mill will take a very strong stand against the idea of creating financial or other structural preferences for anyone based on any kind of inherent characteristic. As an example, you can use their objections to affirmative action–type measures as an example of a "no government interference" position.

PIERUCCI PUBLISHING

Figure 3.

Reasonable people could offer additions to each team, but this I posit is a very representative list. For agreed-to terminology, let's call each separate issue-based group on a team a "platoon." For any Team Right members who might be wondering why I have not included the mainstream media, entertainment industry, academia, or large corporate boardrooms as Team

Left members, the answer is simple. These are not political positions. They are professional positions from which occupants can use the tools of their trade to support team objectives. There are plenty of Team Right journalists, professors, corporate leaders, etc. Team Left has simply done a better job of placing their members inside those various professions.

There is much to cover with regard to how these teams are structured and how they function. As I work through this, please keep in mind that we live under a bell curve. I offer this structure as a working theory that explains the general behavior of people at and near the imaginary mean and a few standard deviations away therefrom. You will certainly know people who do not "fit" into this model (I no longer fit, although I was a Team Right member for decades prior to coming to understand this structure. I then "retired" from team political sports). I would suggest that outliers will, in fact, prove the rule. They will almost exclusively contain people who are highly critical, skeptical, and independent thinkers. Those are not categories into which average citizens generally fall, certainly not *en masse*.

Importantly, I have shown the platoons directly opposite their corresponding counterpart on the other side. That does not mean that they necessarily move in unison, and it certainly does not mean that they rise in prominence and opposition only to the moves of their direct counterparts. Any platoon on any team can suddenly shift and oppose a completely different platoon on the other side.

The first thing to recognize is that these platoons within the teams are built upon ideology, not philosophy. I have a very simple heuristic method for distinguishing between ideology and philosophy. Ideology requires adherence, while philosophy requires application. Ideology requires a person to "hold fast" regardless of circumstances and other considerations. Conversely, philosophy requires that it be applied to circumstances in order to reach the right understanding of what is happening and what to do. Ideology is mindless and rhetorical. Philosophy is thoughtful and questioning. Platoon members on teams are expected to do what their platoon needs to do, and to support their teammates, no matter what. The team structure literally impairs a person's executive function thinking skills and causes them to make decisions on issues reflexively, not thoughtfully.

For those favoring analogies, getting a new idea through to a dedicated platoon member as opposed to a critically thinking non–platoon member is the difference between passing through a heavy set of double doors in an adverse wind versus sliding a screen door on a still summer day.

You would be right to point out that people can belong to more than one platoon, sometimes platoons on different teams at the same time. Does this mean they are on both teams? The short answer is no. When you sit and talk with people and run through a series of "litmus test" issues to determine their opinions (e.g., abortion, capital punishment, tax rates, etc.), what you will find is that people end up identifying with the team that embraces the single-most important issue to them. For example, a person who feels the most important issue to them is a woman's right to choose will tend to become part of Team Left even if they agree with Team Right members on almost every other issue. I have tested this through numerous in-person interviews with differing individuals.

This team membership does something very interesting inside a member's mind when they're confronted with a current event. This is something you can test on yourself anytime you learn of a story in the news that makes you aware of conflict inside your own head as you watch the coverage. Consider this example taken from the Ferguson, Missouri shooting mentioned at the beginning of this chapter.

During the coverage of the event when TV footage depicted mobs rioting in the street and police being the subject of insults and attacks, many people who are not necessarily trusting of police officers and who think the police sometimes go too far in exercising their authority found themselves almost reflexively jumping to the defense of these very same police. Why? Even as they were defending the officers, they (a) didn't know the facts and (b) felt uncomfortable with their own words.

What was likely happening to those people was that they were fellow "team" members of the law and order platoon. Perhaps they were free market supporters and that was why they were on Team Right. If you asked them about the policing policies in large municipalities over a cup of coffee, they might express real personal concern. However, the police (guys on their team) were being threatened by minorities (on the other team) and so they were almost instinctively compelled to support their teammates.

This accounts for some of the unreasonable and seemingly irrational responses of people when issues surface in a news cycle. If I'm on Team Right because of my pro-life position, and if I am a real subject matter expert on the issue, it doesn't mean that I know anything about any other issues. However, when something becomes a big news story, I might find myself arguing strongly in support of my fellow teammates. Since I don't really know much about it, my arguments might come across as being anything from silly to petulant. This behavior will be discussed more in the upcoming chapter of this book.

For example, during the event, I had one prominent political figure reach out to me and say that they had found themselves publicly and aggressively supporting the police and then realized that they still didn't know what had really happened. They caught themselves. They called me to tell me they had fallen into the support-your-teammates trap.

Here you can test yourself. Have you ever found yourself arguing on one side of an issue or news story and realized as you were arguing that you weren't even sure if you really believed in, or agreed with, what you were saying? If that's happened to you, it's likely because you were arguing for your team without even thinking about it. That shouldn't happen. Unfortunately, it happens all too often. When it does happen, it is difficult, if not impossible, to have a rational debate over issues and events.

The groups broken out above represent the core platoons for each team. Each platoon supports the other if it comes into conflict with the other team. When a conflict develops between platoons or members of the same team, you can actually watch the various team leaders create their own "hierarchy" of platoons and it will determine how the entire team processes the conflict. The dynamics of "group think" are never more plainly seen than they are in such circumstances.

Because these teams have been developed over such a long period of time, and because the platoons have become so thoroughly cemented on one team or the other, there is virtually no issue that can come up for discussion that does not involve a platoon for one or both teams. As a result, there is almost nowhere that common ground can be found. Teams play to win whenever they play.

This model can help explain things that otherwise seem either vague and nebulous or simply nonsensical. Take, for example, the phrase we hear often during a political campaign when news reports refer to a candidate as going farther to either the right or the left in their messaging. Under our current terminology, that would mean becoming more fascist or communist. That is not what is happening. What "going farther right or left" really means is that a politician is pandering to more individual platoons on a particular team.

The model also helps to understand how the hierarchy of platoons changes within a team based upon current events and news cycles. When the Ferguson, Missouri incident happened, just like with the George Floyd incident a few years later, Team Left made its "minorities" platoon the most important on the team, and Team Right elevated the "law and order" platoon, jingoistically expressed as "back the blue." Members of other platoons on both teams took a back seat in importance on both occasions. Being a good teammate meant supporting that platoon enthusiastically and without reservation or criticism.

Another interesting aspect of the model is how it is not set in stone and is open to additions. The COVID-19 pandemic is a current and fascinating example. I have written a book about the pandemic and much information can be found elsewhere, but for now, focus on the formation of two new platoons on the two teams: the platoon that favored mandates and vaccinations on one team and the platoon that cried for medical freedom on the other.

Many people have wondered why the pandemic had to become a political issue. After all, shouldn't questions about medicine and public health transcend other political differences that in comparison seem quite pedestrian? The answer is that the team framework is where our country forces every issue. There was never any chance that the pandemic and public health measures would stay above politics. We are built for dichotomy. Very quickly these two oppositional platoons formed, joined their oppositional teams, and were elevated to the status of most important in the competitive game of American politics.

The formation of those platoons and their elevation in importance also created an opportunity to study what it meant to be a "bad teammate" and how those teammates were treated by those wearing the same jersey. No better example exists than that of Dr. Naomi Wolf, the brilliant writer and a leader in the "third wave of feminism."

For decades leading up to the pandemic, Dr. Wolf had not just been a strong Team Left member but had been one of its most respected platoon leaders. As an outspoken feminist, she was a sort of MVP as her platoon moved up and down in team importance over decades based upon what issues were most pressing in any particular moment.

When the pandemic began and new platoons were forming, Dr. Wolf, a brilliant independent mind and critical thinker, began to have serious doubts about the various governmental measures of controls and mandates. She became increasingly convinced of what she perceived as both their ineffectiveness and even potential danger. She started to speak out, and Dr. Wolf has a very loud voice.

How did her fellow Team Left members respond to her critical thinking and its public expression? The answer is through almost universal condemnation and vilification. Dr. Wolf had betrayed her teammates. While the two COVID-generated platoons might have been only newly formed, they had quickly risen to high importance on both teams. For Dr. Wolf to come out against the most important platoon on her team at that moment was treasonous. In a matter of months, those who had previously lauded her work threatened her and condemned her on social media. Over a span of time, Team Left effectively placed Dr. Wolf on waivers and left her to either be claimed by Team Right or to remain a free agent.

You can use the Dr. Naomi Wolf case as an example and apply it to all kinds of people who have had similar public experiences. Also, you can likely see it happen outside of the headlines within your own personal circle, especially if that circle is occupied mostly by members of one of the two teams.

Have you ever experienced having a friend who virtually always agrees with you and others with whom you take a contrary position on an issue that is very "hot" at that moment? What happens often is that the person who breaks orthodoxy finds themselves being excluded from the next dinner gathering.

Dr. Wolf is an exception to the team member structure that proves the rule. When she decided to break ranks and apply her own independent thought and analysis to the pandemic, she effectively had decided to leave a team, whether she realized or not that she had even been a member. Likewise, team members began to renounce her even if they might not understand why they were so doing.

The most important aspect of this team model is that it lets you predict with almost unfailing accuracy what the response will be to any unfolding national situation. Whether it is a new conflict in the Middle East or the latest school shooting, everything is predictable, and that predictability has absolutely nothing to do with right wing–left wing. It has everything to do, however, with Team Right and Team Left.

I mentioned that the military platoons provide a special insight into the team structure. They are, in fact, an example of how the team structure can almost be infiltrated by circumstances and compelling arguments to help fracture it from the inside (which would be a very good thing).

Up until the middle of the last decade, and having held since the Vietnam War, there was a very clear pro- and anti-military platoon on the two teams. One seemed to support the military and its use regardless of the situation, while the other would deride military efforts no matter the threats of the moment. The Team Right support was constructed from the legacy of past American triumph in fighting back against global villains, while Team Left opposition was built upon the inarguable U.S. folly in Vietnam.

Then something happened, but it didn't happen overnight. It happened over a few decades. U.S. involvement in various military escapades around the globe started to raise eyebrows on Team Right. Were these differing missions venturing into conflicts and regions of little, if any, impact to U.S. security interests really necessary? Were they a good way to spend money? Were they a good reason to risk lives? Team Right still remained supportive of the military in general, but they had dropped their pennants and removed their face paint in terms of just being belligerent screaming fans.

On the Team Left side, a couple of things happened. The first was a sort of gradual acquiring of collective guilt over how team members had treated American soldiers coming out of Vietnam. Over time, as it became widely understood just how manipulative and outright evil our political leaders of the time were in commanding those troops, more and more Team Left members came to see that the troops in Vietnam were a special sort of victim. Whatever team members thought about the wrongness of the war, they came to understand that it just wasn't the soldiers' fault. Team Left members came to their own military version of "Hate the sin, love the sinner." A special respect formed for military members, a respect that can be seen on display each year in New York City, where the Bob Woodruff Foundation holds an event called Stand Up for Heroes. It features top-line entertainers and raises money to help wounded veterans. Having personally attended the event each year for over a decade, I can attest to the fact that the theater is filled almost exclusively with Team Left members and that they give a lot of money to show their support not so much for the military, but for its members.

Another change on Team Left occurred after the attacks on our soil on September 11, 2001. The impact was base-level and very natural. Everyone suddenly agreed out loud that the United States needed the capability to defend itself and everyone was glad we had it. How we deployed it over these past 20-plus years is a matter of debate, but gratitude for the capability was nearly universal.

These two platoons are beginning to disappear. What is happening is that they are turning into a sort of blended circle wherein almost all Americans are saying, "I love our military, respect its members, but we need to use it only when vital American interests are at stake." Reasonable people can differ about "vital interests," but having reasonable people differ in today's America is actually our goal. Right now we have unreasonable people competing.

Our political leaders, however, do everything they can to keep us divided on this issue. Our military is a weapon intended to be used on those outside of our borders, whereas our leaders have made it a weapon to use against us. The political leaders are largely ignoring the new unity forming among citizens as to how best to use our military, and they continue to treat soldiers as pawns and foreign conflicts like bank accounts for themselves and large corporations. Why do they do this? Answer below.

NEVER LET A DIVISION GO TO WASTE

The political behavior of these teams is reflected through their general loyalties to either the Republican (Team Right) or the Democratic (Team Left) Party. This is because there are two teams; not three or twenty-seven. Two teams equals two parties for expression. This is an extraordinary failing of the American political system. I would argue that the two-party system is the single-most responsible factor in the division of our country today. It forces complex decisions into a binary structure. This means team conflict finds its strongest manifestation in the voting booth. I say that it is the strongest manifestation because those votes lead to the electing of people who get to pass laws and empower people carrying guns to enforce them. The political leaders nurture this division and preserve the team structure because its binary nature leads to a binary choice on election day: Democrat or Republican. The dissolution of the teams and their being replaced by critically thinking independent members of an electorate would destroy the stranglehold on power the two parties currently enjoy.

To better explain what our leaders are doing to us, I turn to a mind far greater than my own. For anyone seeking to find the true essence of the human experience, there are several different choices. They can read the classic Greek works of Plato and Aristotle. Alternatively, they might read both the Torah and New Testament for a more spiritual take. They might even just try to consume as much Oprah Winfrey content as they can find on cable and YouTube. As for me, I turn always to that great philosopher Theodor Geisel, aka Dr. Seuss.

In his classic tale of the Sneetches, Seuss narrates that there are Sneetches with stars on their bellies (the superior ones) and those without (inferior). This causes resentment and unrest until a fella by the name of McBean comes into town with a machine that puts stars on bellies. Those without "stars on thars" line up quickly and pay for them to be added. Seeing their "star value" lessened, those that had stars originally wanted them removed. McBean could do that, too! What ensued was a free-for-all of Sneetches running through the star-on and star-off machine until McBean ultimately pulled out of town having taken them for all of their money.

This is what has been happening in America with the political leaders, or opportunists, the folks who have ridden into town, like McBean, making promises to fulfill desires. Democrats play to Team Left and Republicans play to Team Right. They put stars on and take stars off in an effort to reach into the pockets or the hearts of regular Americans who have legitimate, perhaps otherwise reconcilable, differences. Philosophers have warned us for centuries about man exploiting man, but their writings are complex. It takes them a while to get to the point. Seuss did it simply and eloquently. . . and with pictures!

Our political leaders and our national opinion leaders do everything they can to keep this American political sport rivalry going. From our conflict and mindless competition with one another, they are able to gain power, privilege, profit, and prestige. They hold power and influence over us by promising to different team members on different platoons that they will fight to help their side win. The dirty little secret is that in a free society, which by definition includes the freedom to hold differing ideas, nobody can ever actually win. There is no final bell or whistle. The best you can ever hope to do is be winning in the moment. The game continues, the nation suffers, and the leaders use our division to drag us farther along the line toward a totalitarian state. I will explain that in the next section.

When people are in conflict, they are open to suggestions. That's because conflict brings with it desperation. The people in this country are living in an almost permanent state of conflict, and it seems as though McBean is making machines on an assembly line. The exploiters are everywhere, and the evidence of their mischief abounds.

THE REAL POLITICAL CONTINUUM

Now I want to examine the second model required to understand the American political landscape and its division—the "real" political continuum. By calling it "real," I mean to say that it objectively exists. People can try to construct other models, either for pseudo-intellectual or propaganda/controlling purposes, but no matter what they construct, there is an actual continuum along which we all move, both as individuals and as a nation, and we ignore it at our own peril.

Consider the representation of the true political continuum shown below:

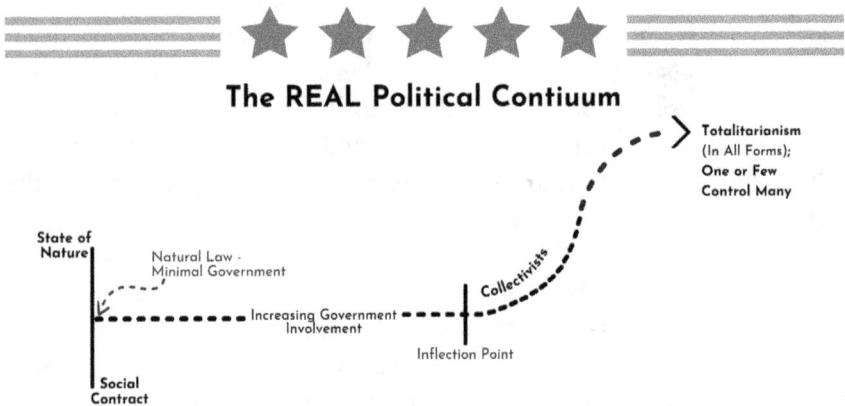

The REAL Political Contiuum

Just outside the far left edge of the continuum, we have the "pre–social contract" period. The idea of a social contract and what people and their lives were like prior to submitting themselves to governance by an authority has been the subject of debate between political philosophers for centuries. For our purposes, that debate is of little interest because whatever the case regarding people's lives in a state of nature, we are certainly beyond that at this point. Let's focus on what happens as we move across the line and into civilized society.

At the far left edge of the continuum is the area that best reflects an environment that embraces the "Natural Law" written about by John Locke, Frédéric Bastiat, and others. As people first consent to be governed, the most proximate form of government to "no government" is one where the only laws recognized as legitimate are those that do the minimum required to protect life, liberty, and property. This type of government would have as little control over the lives of people as possible. In contemporary language, "libertarians" would be the closest defined group as they embrace Natural Law and grant very few, if any, extensions of power beyond that to government. But libertarians have given a political party that name, and since we are trying to change language, let's call people at this far left edge of the political continuum who place individual freedom and limited government at a premium "individualists."

As you move along the political continuum to the right, you are making trade-offs between individual freedom, choice, and responsibility for more government control over areas of life and commerce. Free-thinking and rational individuals can have these types of debates. Each such debate should be framed by using a similar type of question structure:

- How much of our individual privacy are we willing to give up in allowing the government to use surveillance for threat detection?
- How much of our individual income are we willing to part with in order to have a societal safety net for the poor?
- How much personal space are we willing to let police intrude upon in order to search for criminals and prevent potential harm to others?

As we move along this line from left to right, we are deciding to trade individual control for group control. In a modern society, sound arguments can be made that many of these trade-offs are reasonable and beneficial, but all of them need to be viewed in this context and rationally analyzed. If citizens fail to do so, it can lead to crossing the inflection point in the continuum (labeled above as moderates), where granting powers to the government to supplement individual rights changes into the government substituting its power for, and supplanting, individual rights.

Let's call people who believe that a society should be managed beyond that inflection point on the continuum "collectivists." They believe that individual choices are "non-optimizing," and the decisions of a small group, or even an individual, should be imposed upon all individuals collectively within the society for the greater good and for their own good. Of the many problems associated with that point of view, none is more perilous than that of their nicely planned and optimized society slipping rapidly into a more despotic form of control.

Once the inflection point is crossed, once you pass the moderates, a society can very rapidly head toward any one of the many forms of state dominations that have plagued mankind for centuries. No matter the structural form of the suppressing government, regardless of whether or not it has a religious or a secular foundation, no matter if it is ruled by a single person or a "star chamber," the outcome for the general population is always the same: slavery and persecution.

A way to visualize what I'm describing is to think of a treadmill with the side that is colored fully green (for individualists) and the bottom side showing fully gold (for collectivists). As you very slowly start to walk on the treadmill, moving away from fully green showing to a mix of green and gold, you are gradually giving away some individual liberty for more collective control. Eventually, that treadmill runner at your feet will be exactly half green and half gold.

Then, however, something happens. Without you touching the controls, the treadmill speeds up. Gold starts to appear faster and green disappears. Then the treadmill slams to a sudden halt. Only gold is showing, and the treadmill is jammed. End of workout. End of individual liberty.

If it were possible to make every person in the United States today understand what was just explained above, we could immediately begin to make progress on solving problems and addressing issues. It wouldn't magically make everyone want to work together (some people genuinely live and think beyond that inflection point, and they want to actively attain power and control over other people). However, what it would do is clearly expose the motives of those seeking power and control and reveal them for what they really are: collectivists. Citizens on both teams could point at the political continuum and say, "That person who just spoke is far to the right. Let's be careful of them."

It is interesting to note that when I present this model to audiences and ask them where they think America is on the continuum, they almost invariably indicate that we are at or past the inflection point. That should be a wake-up call to everyone. Where do *you* think we are?

PULLING IT ALL TOGETHER

Let's bring the team structure together with the real political continuum and show why these two models need to be taken together and why our current method of communicating is so dangerous and misinformed. First I want to summarize some of the key points about the continuum:

- Individualists are people who primarily embrace Natural law, knowingly or otherwise, and want minimal, if any, government intervention that goes beyond rules protecting life, liberty, and property.
- Collectivists are people who believe that decisions made by a few for the many will be more optimal; serve the greater good; and, self-servingly if they want to be in control, provide them with power and prestige.
- As you move away from strict adherence to Natural Law, you incur trade-offs between individual freedom and more group control.
- There is an inflection point at which so much freedom has been surrendered that additional powers will be granted to the government more swiftly and severely. The process is not a linear one.
- Once you cross that inflection point, it becomes easier for an individual, or a group of individuals, to capitalize on the fact that the people have already surrendered so much freedom that it will be easier to take away the last of it and impose some form of tyranny over everyone.

This progression, which begins at a point of extreme individual liberty at the far left and ends in some form of serfdom at the far right, represents a political continuum that can be used at the macro level to pinpoint the ideological and/or functional location of a nation's population at any moment in time.

Interestingly enough, it can also be used at the micro level to track and understand an individual's life. The farther someone is to the "individualist" side of the spectrum, the more likely they are to be self-reliant and take responsibility for their own lives and actions. If they allow themselves to slide toward the "collectivists" side for their decisions and their outcomes, the more likely they are to become dependent upon others. Dependence leads to becoming susceptible to being victimized, and being victimized leads to being more easily controlled by someone or someones.

IT IS THE SAME FOR A NATION AND ITS PEOPLE.

Our team v. team behavior in this country has led to us taking our eye off the ball in terms of where we are as a nation of free people. We have gotten lost in the flood and have been fighting a fight; one that we can't ever win. We have been exploited by a controlling leadership to be dragged to the right over a very long period of time.

The real danger in not recognizing the two different models is evidenced within the two teams in two different ways. I will take them one at a time.

From a Team Left perspective, there is a tendency if you look closely for Team left members on different platoons to be more willing to use government and lawmaking as a means by which to effect change. What may not be occurring to them is that while they fight for varying policy initiatives that involve government control, they might well be inadvertently and unintentionally sliding us farther to the right on the continuum and providing the opportunity for leaders with collectivism and totalitarian intentions to gain even more power over us. Certainly more power than they intended.

From a Team Right point of view, the overly simplistic construct that Team Left members are "communists" (in quotes because the kinds of communists that Team Right people reference are not actually communists at all; they are simply totalitarians who used good branding; e.g., Lenin, Mao, Castro, etc.) leads them to cast Team Left members as people who want to take away all of their freedom. They should be thinking of them simply as people generally more willing to use government as a means by which to address problems.

The goal for both teams should be to keep the nation as whole somewhere on the flat part of the curve and not to let it cross the inflection point. Should Team Right members contend that it is up to Team Left members not to let that happen because they are the ones generally more willing to use government, then I suggest they need to look in the mirror. It is Team Right members who are largely responsible for one of the greatest threats to our individual liberty present in today's America: federal law enforcement.

The "law and order" platoon sits on Team Right. For decades, that platoon has almost belligerently supported people in law enforcement (as in the Ferguson, Missouri case mentioned in the beginning). That blind support has allowed the size and power of federal law enforcement agencies to grow almost unchecked over time. Today, we see it being turned on Team Right members with regard to the fallacious January 6th insurrection. As Team Right members cry out about their unjust persecution, they would do well to remember that they helped build this monster; and it is a monster. Now it is out of control and able to be utilized by whatever party is in power for its own controlling purposes. When it comes to limiting government power, Shakespeare might well have written, "Team Right member, heal thyself."

It is not just nefarious political and opinion leaders who are taking advantage of the team structure; the individual platoons on each team create the need for platoon leadership. The people that step into those roles are typically zealots and represent the most extreme and activist-oriented element of that platoon. That means they try to be confrontational and outrageous in their behaviors and statements for the purpose of ginning up a mob mentality. Examples of this are everywhere and on both sides.

For America to come together and work to actually solve problems and constructively address issues, the team structure has to be dismantled. That can only happen through rational engagement, and by trying to change platoons into pooled, open forums of honest discussion and problem solving.

Right now it is hard to reach people and get them to understand new ideas because not only are they on a team and taking their team's position, they likely don't even realize they are on that team! These people need to be reorientated in terms of how they think about the entire political landscape. The starting point with this is to ask them one very basic and critical question (included in the following writing prompt):

"In general, do you believe that individuals should be primarily responsible for themselves with little or no help or restrictions from groups or government, or do you believe that groups or the government should be making decisions for individuals and limiting their actions whenever they think it's in the best interest of everyone?"

When they answer that question, you will be able to tell where they are starting from on the political continuum. That gives you one valuable data point.

Next, you need to ask people what issues really matter to them, where they stand on those issues, and why. Remember the hierarchy process discussed earlier that influences what "team" people join. I once interviewed a middle-aged businesswoman and went through a list of eighteen issues to see where she stood. On seventeen out of eighteen, she landed where one would expect a Team Right member to land. On the issue of abortion, however, she felt strongly about a woman's right to choose and said that she would never vote for any Republican because of that. The idea with a person like that isn't to get them to switch teams; it is to get them to abandon the teams altogether. Do that with enough people, and the entire world can change.

The very existence of the team structure makes it emotionally hard for people to leave. Have you ever gone to a party with friends where they knew everyone and you didn't? Remember how it felt when they abandoned you at the door and you felt completely alone and out of place? That's how people feel now when they find themselves dropped in with the other team. Remember, they have been competing with those people! This can't change until the teams are destroyed completely and people begin to look at every issue from the simple perspective of:

How much of my individual freedom am I willing to give up in order to address and solve this problem?

So what you need to do at every opportunity, in every engagement you have with people discussing politics, economics, and issues, is simple:

- Challenge their use of terms and phrases.
- Make them tell you what their terms and phrases mean.
- When they show you they don't understand, then you show them what's true!

It is my opinion that we are well on the road toward totalitarianism in the United States. I believe that the models I have shared, along with the historical background, clearly identify that as our likely future. Starting with Dickens, every novel written or movie filmed that involves people traveling into the future ultimately addresses the same question: Are they seeing things that will be or that might be? As you observe the United States becoming increasingly fractured in the fight between Team Left and Team Right, and drifting farther along the curve away from the individualist side to the collectivist side, that is the question you should be asking. It is also the issue you should be trying to address with every intellectual weapon you possess. The country's future, and with it the future of individual freedom, hangs in the balance.

On Christmas Eve in 1914, during World War I, Allied soldiers joined their German counterparts in doing something spontaneously that had been formally rejected by military leadership on both sides. Soldiers from both sides left their trenches and journeyed into "no-man's-land," that area in between the trenches more commonly occupied by the barbed wire and the bodies of their fallen comrades. For the next few days, they sang songs together, played games, exchanged gifts, and shared a wartime celebration of Christmas. It was a sort of miracle. It showed what could be.

Unfortunately, after Christmas, the two sides returned to their trenches and kept killing each other for four more years.

The space between Team Right and Team Left in this country has become a sort of modern American no-man's-land. Regular citizens don't know how to get there, and our political and opinion leaders don't want you to go there. They want you to keep fighting. Let me suggest to you that it is time for a random act of civil disobedience. In defiance of your team platoon leaders, in defiance of your political leaders, in defiance perhaps of your own instincts, I implore you to step out of the trenches and don't go back in. Turn America's no-man's-land into one of common ground.

TAKE THE "LEFT-RIGHT NEWS CHALLENGE"

Spend a week while watching or reading the news, across a good cross-sample of outlets, and use your computer tablet to make notes of every reference to the terms "right" or "left" when used in a political context. Note what issue was being discussed and what opinion or attribute was connected to the right or the left label. Also note whether the person was using it in a favorable, unfavorable, or neutral way. At the end of the week, sort and review your notes and see if you can draw any solid conclusions about what the terms mean and the consistency of their use.

PROMPTS TO REFLECT ON CHAPTER ONE

Pick up a newspaper or two and identify 3–5 headlines that pander to the "right-left" language division.

_____

_____

_____

_____

_____

What platoons do you think exist but were not identified in the text? Defend your position.

_____

_____

_____

_____

What team are you on and why?

_____

_____

_____

_____

_____

Reflect upon what team you might be classified under, and why? What views do you hold that would traditionally qualify for the opposing side?

_____

_____

_____

_____

_____

Where do you think America is on the continuum?

_____

_____

_____

_____

_____

Come up with a plan for engaging someone on the other team and sharing this structure. See where they think are.

_____

_____

_____

_____

_____

Do you agree with the author that we are well on the road to totalitarianism in the United States? Why or why not?

_____

_____

_____

_____

_____

CHAPTER TWO:

AN IDEA FOR HEALING OUR PERSONAL DIVISIONS

"Conversation should be pleasant without scurrility, witty without affectation, free without indecency, learned without conceitedness, novel without falsehood."
—*William Shakespeare*

In 2015, after I wrote "How America Broke Its Wings—The Causes and Effects of the Right-Left Divide and How to Repair It" (Turning Point USA, 2015), the previous chapter in this collection, which analyzed the historical roots of America's current division, I was asked by some to take that macro-level work down to the individual micro level and explain what has gone wrong in terms of individual communication and engagement and how to repair it.

In light of what has happened over the intervening years since this was first written, I thought about almost a full rewrite to include events such as the pandemic, the 2020 election controversy, and the crisis of the moment, which is the warfare in the Middle East and Ukraine. After reviewing it, however, I decided that nothing really needed to be changed materially as the examples still hold in support of the contentions, and the principles are timeless. If anything, I feel this offering is even more needed today than it was back in 2018 when it was first penned and published by me on LinkedIn.

My greatest personal revelation in the intervening five years is that the key to changing the world and restoring civility lies in the simple reversal of two tiny words. If we can replace the declarative "it is" with the interrogative "is it," we can have a profound impact upon our receptiveness and that of others. Please read what follows with that new thought paradigm in mind.

When my friend and partner Felisa Blazek launched the Common Ground Campus program in 2022, I had the opportunity to observe firsthand

and interactively how these communication breakdowns actually take place. I was also given the opportunity through the program to help solve the problem by sharing some of these kinds of ideas with the most important people in our country—our youth.

This chapter is for the benefit of each and every American citizen. Regardless of your personal attributes, regardless of your race or religion, and regardless of your politics, we all stand on the precipice of losing our liberty because we can no longer have a simple conversation. You are asked to read, you are asked to consider, you are asked to converse.

FROM 30,000 FEET–A LOOK

AT THE PROBLEM

Whether it is through viewing any social media platform, turning on a cable news channel, talking with a friend at a coffee shop, or even sitting down to dinner with family, evidence clearly shows that Americans are finding it increasingly difficult to have a civil and productive issue-based conversation. Take a moment and think:

Have you ever found yourself talking to someone with whom you "agree" and discussing how people can't converse rationally anymore, and then sometime later you find yourself in a shouting match with someone with whom you "disagree"?

What's going on?

Everyone laments about how our politicians can't get anything done in Washington (or in most states, for that matter). The problem isn't the politicians. In a very real sense, they are getting something done every day. They are maintaining their positions of power, privilege, and prestige because all of us as citizens are so busy fighting with each other we can't come together long enough to stop them. If we have any hope of being able to come together to take back control of our government and our liberty, we have to understand why we are constantly fighting, instead of discussing, with people who disagree with us.

This isn't completely, or even mostly, a problem of either ideology or philosophy. This is an internal data processing problem and an external communication problem. I want to try and generate awareness on the part of the reader as to what is taking place, so that this awareness can help change the way you interact with others. Our nation is dying due to a lack of constructive engagement.

You will notice:

At any moment during any day of the week, you can turn on one of the various cable news networks and find two people arguing. Now these people can be arguing about abortion rights, gun control, climate change, or any of a near infinite number of issues on which positions are commonly and quite predictably staked out by Team Right and Team Left members.

These point-counterpoint discussions have become so cacophonous that they are difficult to watch. Since the January 2017 Trump Presidential Inauguration, a self-imposed pledge of television news celibacy to protest the removal of "news journalism" from the term "cable news journalism" has only reinforced the conclusions reached herein. That personal withdrawal notwithstanding, if you Google any of the participants in these verbal cage matches, you will find some interesting commonalities.

Both/any/all of the participants you will find to be educated, along with having some measure of achievement and recognized subject matter expertise in their background. You will likely find YouTube clips of them arguing their position with lots of "likes" and a string of passionate and vitriolic comments trailing. They will be published authors and contributors to various media outlets. All available evidence will indicate these sparring partners to be qualified and knowledgeable. And yet . . .

They don't agree. Not only do they not agree, but they don't agree with such a level of certainty and insistence to the opposing party that they are "wrong" that it leads you to believe that they are both: ·

- Idiots (but they aren't).
- Being paid to simply take opposing views they don't even believe in (hopefully not).
- Ignoring all facts and just sharing how they feel (maybe on Jerry Springer—not here).

- Right and wrong at the same time (unlikely except to existentialists).

What goes on between those guests who are being viewed by some significant number of people (and in high definition with Dolby Surround Sound) is a microcosm of what is going on every day, all around the country, between millions of people arguing with one another. People aren't screaming at each other because they think they themselves are wrong but want to convince others nonetheless. Rather, they are as certain of the correctness of their position as is their opponent.

How this happens is more process oriented than it is individual awareness and choice oriented. What follows is a dissection of the typical process, hopefully leading to reader awareness through which a path can emerge to change behavior.

MYTH: "THERE ARE TWO SIDES TO EVERYTHING."

This simple little maxim is offered under the auspices of showing tolerance (long before tolerance was a tool of political correctness). The idea is that if someone comes to your door and rants for fifteen minutes about the behavior of their stepsister, that stepsister would have her own fifteen-minute rant that's completely different but equally important.

The problem is that this simple maxim is geometrically incorrect and effectively crippling to social discourse.

When someone uses the "two sides" phrase, they are either wittingly or unwittingly introducing moral relativism into the conversation. The clear intention is to acknowledge and validate both participants in the dispute and to conclude, in essence, that neither is actually right or wrong but that, from their view, they are both equally right and truthful. It is as if the truth, itself, is unknowable; therefore, we have to take each at their word and have them simply agree to disagree. The quest for clarity comes to a screeching halt

But what is really being said when we say there are two sides? We are saying that there are two different perspectives from which the situation is being viewed and described. Given that we learned in geometry that there are an infinite number of potential "sides" to any hypothetical object, the potential number of sides to any issue is entirely dependent upon the number of viewers or participants. Each participant would have their own perspective, which equates to their side. The number of sides is limited only by the number of humans inhabiting the planet.

The problem is found not so much in the number of sides to a situation under discussion; the problem is in granting equal standing to all of those sides simply because, from the viewer's perspective, the sides exist. There is a deliberate trivialization of the role of facts in the situation under discussion because of the unjustified emphasis on sides. Problem resolution and agreement become next to impossible because there is no way to clearly focus upon the underlying core problem.

One of the great problems with Critical Theory and all of its subsequent derivatives is that it places the emphasis on subjective personal perspectives instead of objective facts. This creates a problem because the truth, of course, is that while there are an infinite number of sides, there is only a single, finite set of facts.

MY FACTS, YOUR FACTS, OUR FACTS, NO FACTS

Facts are interesting and nettlesome things. As you listen to others argue, notice some of the references and idiomatic phrases that are used regarding facts:

"You have your facts, I have mine."
"That's not what the facts are."
"There are lies, damned lies, and statistics."
"They've done research that says . . ."
"The plain, simple fact of the matter is "
"Look, facts are facts."
This list is intended to offer a sampling, not a universe.

Facts are pesky. They get in the way of someone being able to quickly advance the correctness of their side. The issues presented by facts that make them so troubling are:

- You don't usually know how many there are
- You don't know where to find all of them.
- It is time-consuming to pursue them.
- They may not help support your opinion of the issue once you do find them (more on opinions later).

- You aren't certain if you can trust them when you find them (a common problem with the mislabeling of facts that is addressed further herein). Artificial intelligence has only served to compound this problem and it is going to continue to get worse.

The one known element about facts in any situation is that, unlike sides, which come from the aggregate number of participants, there are a finite number of them. They exist objectively. There might be ten or there might be a thousand. Regardless, there is a certain sum of facts.

PERSPECTIVE, PREJUDICE, AND NOISE . . .

Now imagine two well-intentioned participants with differing opinions regarding a particular event. They set a time to discuss their issue with one another for 2:00 p.m. the day after tomorrow. In the meantime, they want to be fully informed with facts before the discussion begins. They are determined to have a fact-based conversation. So they both set out on their own individual quest for facts.

Over the next two days, both of them will learn different things. Assuming they are able to uncover only true facts and are not diverted by "noise" (to be discussed later), when they sit down together for their 2:00 p.m. showdown, the likely scenario regarding the two of them and the facts are that:

- Each of them found facts the other didn't find.
- They both found some of the same facts.
- Some facts remained undiscovered by both of them.

Now, if our two participants are able to sit down and stick only to the facts, there is both good news and bad news. The good news is that they will be able to take what they have learned separately from each other, share it, and then have a discussion around the complete universe of facts as they have discovered them. The bad news is that no matter how cooperative and well mannered they are, they are still not operating with all the facts. Since that latter point is almost always and unavoidably the case, this would be a realistic best-case, albeit imperfect, scenario for civil and productive conversation about the matter at hand.

Unfortunately, this is almost never the case. Not only is the painstaking investment of time not placed into the discovery of facts, but the problematic factors of perspective, prejudice, and noise likely deteriorate the discussion. Both quality and civility with peaceful resolution are no longer an option.

The next thing to do is to look at the elements of perspective, prejudice, and noise to understand how their presence leads to difficulty in communication and problem solving. Much like someone with an addiction to drugs or alcohol, awareness of the problem is the first step in being able to conquer it.

PERSPECTIVE AND PREJUDICE:

YOUR VANTAGE POINT WITH

OBSTRUCTED VIEWS

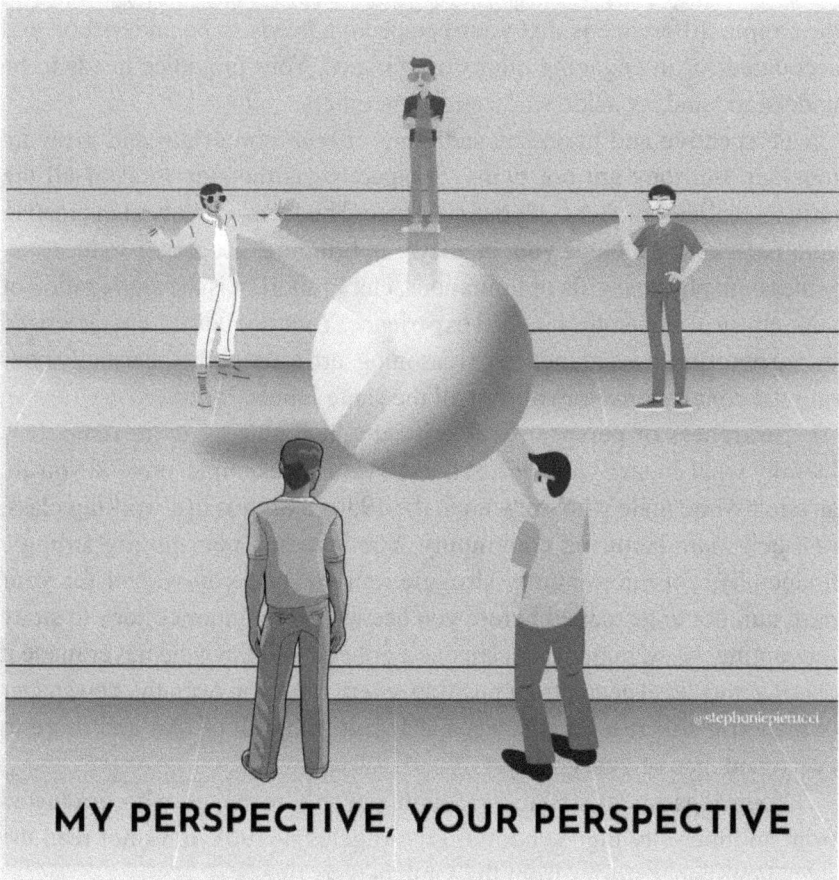

MY PERSPECTIVE, YOUR PERSPECTIVE

A DEFINITION OF PERSPECTIVE

As mentioned earlier, when we say, incorrectly, there are two sides to every story, the "sides" to which we refer are actually perspectives. If we can imagine an issue as being a solid object that is hovering in a central location several feet above the floor, as in Figure 5, then picture numerous observers of the issue scattered around, all perched on differing seats either grounded or themselves hovering. Each observer would then have their own unique perspective of the single solid issue that would become his or her "side" of that issue.

Literally stated, perspective is point of view. We use the phrase "point of view" as a synonym for opinion. This is a misuse of language. Your point of view is the place from which you are viewing the facts of the situation.

Perspective and prejudice can too often be used interchangeably and are confused by people as being synonymous. They aren't. In this context, the simple difference is that your perspective needs to be understood and accounted for in engaging others over issues. Your prejudice needs to be understood and set aside while engaging others.

Perspective and prejudice sadly are of common origin and grow up together, but they are not twins. Perspective is the sum total of all the rational realities, or facts, of your existence. The factors involved in creating your perspective include your ethnicity, upbringing, geography, education, profession, physical gifts or limitations, etc. In short, it is the aggregation of your physical and environmental experience. Your prejudices, characterized by the notoriousness of inductive reasoning, are essentially the usually non-rational conclusions drawn from all the same inputs.

Awareness of perspective is critical when addressing an issue. It is literally what creates your side of the story. As an example, pretend you are an adult white male who grew up in the 1950s and '60s in a working class, rust-belt manufacturing community. You watched your family struggle financially, your community struggle racially, and you waited for your draft number to get called before you headed off to junior college to study accounting. Now, many years later as a gray flannel guy who never made it out of a mid-level accounting position, every time you open the newspaper (which you still read as a newspaper), you bring all of that and more to every sentence of every story.

Your department's Black accounts payable manager, who graduated from an inner-city high school in Los Angeles in 1968, does not read the same newspaper stories from the same perspective.

Your perspective can and does change over the course of your lifetime. Remember, it is an accumulation of environmental influences, and while those have a disproportionate impact in our young and formative years, they do not stop impacting you, especially for those who are of a more aware and introspective nature.

A DEFINITION OF PREJUDICE

Prejudice is differentiated from perspective in the sense that while it came from all of the same life experiences, it takes total leave from the rational and causes vision clouding and image distortion when viewing the central issue from your perspective. Think of perspective as your vision from a certain sightline and prejudice as cataracts.

If you are a white police officer and you come from a legacy family of police officers, your perspective, in part, comes from being behind the badge on matters of law enforcement. Let's say you read a story about the shooting of an Black youth in the inner city by a white police officer. Let's further assume that the facts of the incident are all fully documented with film footage and corroborated by officer and bystander accounts. Finally, assume that, in this case, the facts overwhelmingly indicate that the shooting was not justified.

Your perspective in processing all of this might lead you to conclude that while the officer was wrong to do what he did, there must have been something going on inside his head in those moments surrounding the event that led him to that bad decision. Now, if you had any prejudice regarding Black youth that you developed over time, you might take that above thought from your perspective, add a comma, and say, "But the kid probably had it coming anyway for some other reason."

If you understand that the initial question you asked is coming from your perspective, it is useful. It could lead you to look further into the incident to get a better understanding of what really did, if anything, go through that officer's mind and that awareness could help you prevent the same sort of thing from possibly happening on your watch with your unit. If, however, you don't check the prejudice you brought to the viewing of the event, then you will never gain any insightful knowledge from the experience. You won't even bother to look. No possible future change can take place.

In a perfect theoretical framework, you would in every instance remove both perspective and prejudice and place yourself directly inside the issue, surrounded only by facts and unencumbered by any artificial or superficial filters. The problem is that we do not live with the ability to jettison our life and experiences from every circumstance; or from any, for that matter. The focus, therefore, needs to be on personal awareness and intellectual vigilance.

As previously stated, prejudice and inductive reasoning are connected. It is important to understand that prejudice, at its lowest common denominator, is nothing more than applied (often misapplied) inductive reasoning. Inductive reasoning is characterized by the drawing of a conclusion about the next item or event after having previously viewed some number of related items or events.

As an example, if you watch traffic lights around the country, you will see a pattern of the light moving from green to yellow to red, and then repeating the cycle. The pattern is general and constant, and is universal throughout the country. Any driver knows that red means stop, green means go, and yellow means go fast.

The problem of too much reliance upon inductive reasoning is this: Imagine you are at a traffic light waiting for it to change from red to green. You see cars starting to slow down as they approach the intersection from your left and right. You assume, using inductive reasoning, that the light is about to turn green. As you preemptively ease out into the intersection, you are nearly sideswiped by an oncoming emergency vehicle that failed to successfully change the lights. Your inductive logic, your prejudice toward traffic light behavior, could have gotten you killed.

The traffic light example shows how the use of induction, or prejudice, can be dangerous even when it is well founded (it is highly likely that lights will change from red to green). The prejudice factor becomes even worse when it is built upon faulty data. Anyone reading this can quickly call to mind the types of false, general conclusions that people routinely draw about other people or circumstances. They often start with words such as "None of them ever . . . ," or "Those people can't . . . ," or "Anyone who believes that is . . . " When you start to hear those words coming out of yourself or others, you will know that prejudice has likely just raised its ugly head and entered the conversation.

For anyone who doubts the dangers of prejudice in leading to wrong decisions, ask yourself this: Have you ever had an email that was *not* spam end up in your spam folder? All users of email have had this happen. Email uses something called a Bayesian filter based on the inductive logic developed by the English mathematician Thomas Bayes. This filter is designed to look for keywords and calculate the probability that the message is, in fact, spam. Sadly, every once in a while the valid email gets creamed at the in-box intersection.

When I originally wrote this piece in 2018, the nation was in the midst of the Senate hearings regarding the potential confirmation of Judge Brett Kavanaugh to the U.S. Supreme Court. The accusations of sexual misconduct that surfaced late in the proceedings were preoccupying the attention of the American media and all social media platforms.

Without knowing the facts as of yet, or the eventual outcome of the process, what was clearly evident was the role that prejudice was playing in the discussions. The most extreme example of this was a video released by a collection of female Hollywood celebrities in support of the accuser. The script from that video reads, in part:

We applaud your courage in coming forward for the public good, and we will be with you as you face the inevitable backlash. You are strong. And you are not alone. You are a survivor. Millions of us have your back. You and your testimony are credible. We believe you. . . . Signed, Your sisters.

As a by-product of the #MeToo movement, these women were clearly operating from a personal prejudice that led them to conclude that any accusation of sexual misconduct made by any woman against any man is not just credible, but true. While Kavanaugh was eventually confirmed in July 2018, the lesson of the perverting effect that prejudice and bias can have on the process of rational circumstantial analysis cannot be made more visually clear than it has been in this referenced video.

Prejudice does have a bad name that isn't entirely justified. It is prejudice that stops you from going into a small carryout restaurant because the last four people you know who ate there all got sick. That's prejudice; that's inductive reasoning. Employing inductive reasoning is how we function through most of our day. In routine circumstances it is often reliable and its misuse doesn't usually lead to fatal errors. However, when it is introduced into a discussion about political issues, it almost without exception nullifies fact-based, solution-driven conversation.

HEARING THROUGH THE NOISE:
FACTS WHISPER, BUT FANCY SCREAMS

The above section makes clear the barriers to communication that each of us carries inside us. Perspective and prejudice are intrinsic to our very being and impact every conversation we have. We have no hope of ever eliminating them because they are human traits and we are all very human. The best we can hope for is a level of awareness that renders our perspective neutral and holds our prejudice at bay.

That would be difficult enough if it were the only thing we needed to do in order to have informed, positive, and agreement-building conversations with other people. Unfortunately, those aren't the only impediments. The other barrier to civil public discourse is one that is external to us. For the purpose of this discussion, let's call it noise.

Noise is the thick layer of insulation that is wrapped around facts. It takes many forms. Opinion pieces in "print" can be noisy. The inaccurate or incomplete reporting of facts can be noise. The deliberate presentation of untruths as facts can be noise. Virtually everything found on X and other social media platforms is noise. It seems as though you can trust none of what you hear and less of what you see.

In short, "noise" is anything designed to misrepresent a fact, or shape and characterize a fact in a manner that makes it more difficult for the fact-searcher to find it, recognize it, or understand it.

One could argue that we had never before seen such rapidly spreading disinformation as we did during the 2016 presidential election campaign. The things that were posted about each candidate, most with only shreds of truth at best and nearly all in a vitriolic format, created such a high level of noise that it was almost impossible to find out if anything that was being said or alleged was true. There were so many allegations and stories that to get to the truth for any one person on any one "tweet" would have been laborious and time-consuming.

Most people didn't even try. They simply looked for things that fit their own thought paradigm (referred to as confirmation bias) and retweeted them with the import and implication of fact. But they weren't. They were noisy. During that 2016 presidential campaign, noise was present everywhere, including through established news sources, but was especially prevalent in social media. That leads to another problem with noise: There is more of it than there is fact.

As previously mentioned, noise wraps around facts like insulation. Sadly, not only is there more of it and not only does it wrap around the facts, but it is pervasive. In this day and age, it is virtually impossible to turn to any particular source of information and have it be only factual. Noise is frequently presented as fact by people and organizations that the citizens desperately want to trust. Older readers will remember when CBS News Anchorman Walter Cronkite was called the most trusted man in America. Well, not only was Cronkite not trustworthy in his time (by his own admission, he altered the presentation of facts relating to the Tet Offensive in the Vietnam War), but today with the proliferation of news outlets, there are hundreds, if not thousands, of people whom Americans want to trust, but shouldn't.

In September 2018, the *New York Times*, still considered by many to be the "paper of record" in the United States, reported a story wherein the headline and the associated photograph suggested that U.N. Ambassador Nikki Haley and her office had spent $52,000 on draperies. Unfortunately, the apparent "fact" wasn't a fact at all. It was only disclosed later in the story that the draperies had been ordered under the previous administration. The headline created a firestorm on social media both from people who are opposed to government waste, and from others who simply oppose all things related to the Trump Administration. The correction issued by the *Times* the next day did not receive the same recognition and fanfare. Noise lives.

There are numerous other examples of the conflation of facts and noise. The "Russia investigation," which commenced in 2017, has had as a by-product so much noise that it is almost impossible to discuss the matter with anyone and find the truth in their underlying assertions. In one extreme case, the writer sat with a learned and nationally respected attorney who ran off a litany of "facts" about the matter over lunch. Curious, the writer did some internet research and discovered that of five "facts" cited, three were rumored speculation and two were actually provably false.

The noise can sometimes be deafening. The noise is always defeating when it comes to problem solving.

When citizens pick up larger amounts of noise than facts, and then they view that noise from their perspective and infuse their own prejudice, something quite predictable happens: They get noisy, literally. It is almost invariable that the loudest shouter in the room, or the vilest poster on Facebook, is the person who is heavily armed with noise and not facts, has no idea regarding the nature of their own perspective, and has fully embraced their own personal prejudices. You cannot question them, you cannot reason with them, and you can't get the umber coloring to leave their cheeks.

So, having identified the impediments to rational conversation that are within us (perspective and prejudice), and an impediment that is external to us (noise), it is time to introduce a simple and common synthesis of the two that nearly everyone in a political conversation is guilty of creating. At first glance it will seem harmless, and at first thought it will appear necessary. My promise to you is that it can be proven to be neither, and just two simple examples will show you how it has the power to tear a nation, let alone a conversation, apart.

THE PERILS OF PARAPHRASING

As we all know, paraphrasing is the technique of restating someone's words, to attain some brevity and greater clarity. Conversationally, we often introduce a paraphrase by saying, "In other words . . ." or by saying, "What he/she means by that is . . ." The original statement is then remade with new words, the intention being to just make sure things are clear.

In everyday conversation this is a very useful, indeed necessary, tool. Much would be missed if people were always left only with the original utterance. The problem with the use of paraphrasing in political discourse is that, more often than not, it contributes to the level of noise which then falls into the waiting arms of perspective and prejudice.

When Donald Trump declared his candidacy for president in 2015, his speech included an attack on the current immigration system in the United States. He would go on to make that a central theme of his entire campaign right up through the general election.

Trump's speech touched off a firestorm because of the following lines (this is lifted from the actual transcript):

> *"Thank you. It's true, and these are the best and the finest. When Mexico sends its people, they're not sending their best. They're not sending you. They're not sending you. They're sending people that have lots of problems, and they're bringing those problems with us. They're bringing drugs. They're bringing crime. They're rapists. And some, I assume, are good people."*

Immediately after Trump's speech, newspeople, commentators, and politicians from both teams effusively denounced Trump for saying that "Mexican immigrants are rapists and drug addicts." Of course, that isn't what Trump said. They were paraphrasing. Shortly after the speech, when questioned about the remarks, Trump repeatedly clarified that he was referring to the Mexican government. It didn't matter. The paraphrase lived and it continues to live. I heard someone in conversation just a few days before this was typed referring to the same quote (which, of course, isn't a quote).

There is some evidence that the Mexican government has facilitated or encouraged the "exporting" of undesirables from their country to ours. When you point out to someone what was actually said and then how it was subsequently fully clarified, the typical response is, "It doesn't matter. We all know what he meant." While this analysis has nothing whatsoever to do with defending or criticizing Donald Trump in particular, you have to ask yourself: How can it not matter and how do you really know what he meant?

Once people took Trump's words, paraphrased them, and introduced them into public discourse, the paraphrasing became noise. It became the kind of noise that people were either accidentally or purposefully adding to their list of facts. Once noise gets itself so closely attached to real facts, it behaves a bit like a tick under a dog's collar. The noise becomes so attached that its simple removal is painful and bloody to the host.

Since we have introduced Donald Trump into the discussion, let's use another example that is often referenced in conversations at the time of this writing.

On August 12, 2017, Donald Trump stood up at his private golf club in Bedminster, New Jersey, to address the violence that had just erupted out of a protest rally in Charlottesville, Virginia. In what were brief remarks at the time, Trump said, "We're closely following the terrible events unfolding in Charlottesville, Virginia. We condemn in the strongest possible terms this egregious display of hatred, bigotry, and violence. On many sides."

What actually happened on August 12 was that a rally entitled "Unite the Right," which was organized by a man associated with white supremacy positions, wound up in confrontation with a group of counterprotesters, in part organized by a group known as "ANTIFA" (short for anti-fascists). As the words and tension heightened between the two sides, a member of the organizing "team" got into his car and plowed into the crowd, killing a young woman counterprotester.

Trump's remarks were instantly paraphrased through all forms of media, and by politicians, as "equating" the white racist antagonists with well-meaning, open-minded protesters. That isn't what he said, and it isn't what the facts presented. It didn't make any difference. The paraphrase was born; it was converted into a "quote." It became added to the noise surrounding the actual facts, and national outrage ensued. The next day, Trump was forced to clarify his remarks to which the anticipated response was: "It doesn't matter. We know what he meant."

The *New York Times*, just on its own, had to issue five corrections for misquoting what Trump said. It doesn't matter. The paraphrase joined the swirling universe of noise and provided an insulating wrap around the facts.

This paraphrasing problem is not a Team Left or a Team Right problem. It is a human problem. The combination of people's busy lives and varying degrees of intellectual laziness are the two greatest contributors to both the creation of the paraphrase and to its being repeated as fact. Paraphrasing is not just limited to specific words and statements; it also applies to ideas. After the shooting of Michael Brown in Ferguson, Missouri by a local police officer, if a person conjectured for a variety of factual reasons that perhaps the shooting was justified despite Brown's unarmed status, they may have found their speculations reduced to "he doesn't care if the cops shoot black people."

Please permit a quick digression back to the concept of noise and its creation from the events of Ferguson. One of the earliest reports of the incident that appeared in the press was an eyewitness account of the event that had the shooting victim, Michael Brown, putting his hands in the air and saying to the police officer, "Don't shoot." According to the account, the officer shot Brown anyway. After a very thorough investigation by the Obama Administration's Justice Department, it was determined that this account of the incident was false. It didn't matter.

The term "Hands up. Don't shoot" has been used by NBA players, celebrities, politicians, and protesters ever since. To many, that is exactly what happened that night in Ferguson even though investigations proved that it didn't. There are people reading this who are now stopping mid-sentence to refer to Google to see if what they are reading can possibly be true because they had been sure the "facts" were otherwise. All hail the power of noise.

Returning to paraphrasing, while it is often done out of laziness or time limits, it is also often done because of a need to make something fit with a pre-formed opinion of the paraphraser. Opinions are essentially the last step, the outcome if you will, of this communication process. So let's examine opinions.

ALL OPINIONS ARE NOT CREATED EQUAL!

"Everyone is entitled to their opinion." This little dandy of idiomatic speech is absolutely correct and positively irrelevant to productive discourse. It is true that there is no law (yet) that prevents anyone from holding an opinion about anything; nor should there be. The problem is that because everyone is entitled to have one, we have made that synonymous with saying that everyone's opinion should be valued and respected. This just simply isn't the case.

Opinion is something that should come at the end of an analysis of the facts of a situation. Its drivers need to be philosophy (an individual's overall contextual paradigm which they apply to mankind), ethics (the value judgments of right and wrong, good and evil, etc.), and empirical knowledge and evidence collected over time. In applying those and arriving at an opinion, a person needs to be conscious of how their perspective has influenced their opinion formation, and they need to remove their prejudice from the opinion-creating process.

Of course, this is not how opinions are commonly formed, and therein we find one of the biggest problems with civil and productive political conversations.

When an opinion is properly constructed, it should be a one-off for the particular situation being considered. Every incident has its own unique set of facts. Those facts need to be taken in systematically; through a process (see below). For any one individual, the application of this process would inherently lead to a "consistency" of opinions because they would be applying the same method and tools to the review of every matter before them.

The problem is that not only do people not form their opinions using that method, but they often bring their opinions with them as they head into a situational analysis. In this sense, they are essentially overlaying them onto a unique set of facts prior to going through the evaluation process.

There are two expressions that are commonly used interchangeably that shouldn't be. The first is, "Your opinion doesn't fit the facts." The second is, "Your opinion isn't supported by the facts." The first is a non sequitur, given how opinions should be formed only at the end of an analysis process.

Opinions fitting facts imply that they already existed prior to the circumstance and then an attempt was made to wrap them around the situation. A very common example of this is when a person doesn't care for a particular politician and a friend might say, "No matter what they do, you aren't going to agree with it." When this statement is true about someone, it is an example of trying to fit opinions into facts as opposed to deriving opinions from facts.

It is counterintuitive, but the truth is that when someone lays their opinion over the facts, they actually end up coming across as being inconsistent rather than consistent. Why? The reason is that the one-size-fits-all of opinions to facts doesn't work. Each set of facts is unique so, to the informed listener, the person who starts with an opinion will end up saying some of the most incredulous things about a particular circumstance. This is another reason why following the proper process to arrive at opinions is so important.

Here is how the process should work:

Event > Gather facts > Analyze with Reason and Philosophy > Form Opinion

In America today, here is what too many people are too often doing:

Event > Apply Our Bias > Form Our Opinion > Find Facts to Support Opinion

Sadly, most people will accept the assertion of a "fact" if it supports their preformed opinion. Conversely, they are just as likely to reject the assertion of a fact if it refutes their preformed opinion.

When someone does follow the proper process but their opinion isn't necessarily supported by the facts, we have an opportunity for real conversation and resolution. It could be that there has been faulty analysis of the situation caused by any one or more of the variables previously mentioned. This is resolvable. Two people walking through the process of how each arrived at their differing opinions could determine if either of them had made a "mistake" along the way. If not, then we know that the difference is the result of philosophy, ethics, and empiricism in some form or combination. The two could then try to work toward compromise.

One of the reasons we get thrown off course by opinions is that we don't stop to consider that, within the process of opinion formation, there are actually different types of opinions that are being formed. Because people use the word "opinion" in general, they don't take into account whether the opinion is regarding the subjective, or is it an opinion regarding the objective?

Let's introduce the terms "subjective opinions" and "objective opinions." In this context, a subjective opinion is one that is not supported by, nor does it require the support of, any underlying fact or set of facts to be offered into discussion. An objective opinion is one that does require such support in order for it to be offered into discussion.

To illustrate, let's take the idiomatic phrase "Beauty is in the eye of the beholder." To be politically incorrect for a moment, if ten men are watching the Miss Universe Pageant and it is down to the two finalists, Ms. Brazil and Ms. China, if nine of those ten men say that Ms. China is the fairest of the two and only one of them says that the nod in that regard goes to Ms. Brazil, is the other nine men's opinion more "correct"? Of course not. While they may be in a majority, their idea of beauty is no more valid than the lone man cheering on Ms. Brazil. In his opinion, Ms. Brazil is more beautiful and you cannot in any way fault his reasoning or thought process.

In much the same way, if a seventeen year-old moviegoer sees a film just badly panned by a *New York Times* theater critic and says it's the greatest film ever, his opinion is every bit as valid as the critic's. There is no objective standard. There are no facts. Entertainment, like beauty, is in the eye of the beholder.

So in the realm of the purely subjective, anybody's opinion is just as "valid" as anyone else's. Much of what we encounter every day falls into this category. "This is the best pizza anywhere," "Football is better than baseball," "*Gone with the Wind* crushes *Citizen Kane*." These are all examples of common conversation themes where opinion differences are subjective and, generally speaking, fun. Granted, even conversations over pizza and sports can get fairly heated, but when they do, they usually de-escalate relatively quickly.

The problem is that since we spend so much time on subjective opinion discussion, we don't realize when the conversation shifts to opinions over objective facts and events. In these situations, the opinion holder has an obligation to themselves and to others to work through a diligent process of opinion formation. Since they usually don't, these conversations rapidly deteriorate, and unlike disagreements over the relative value of baseball and football, these differences lead to fractured social structures.

Imagine two university students sitting down in a coffee shop, one a PhD candidate who for years has been studying all of the original texts surrounding America's founding documents, the other a freshman who has only had a high school American history class and has done no outside reading. They decide to share their opinions over America's Founding Fathers and their underlying intentions. The idea that the opinion of each is of the same value is preposterous. Yet we fall into this trap all the time. Doing so cheapens the value of knowledge and increases the likelihood of poor fact analysis because the opinion holder, who has not invested the time into the proper formation process, learns quickly that nobody cares.

You don't have to work at having an opinion supported by facts; you can just form your opinion and wrap it around the facts (to the extent you even know any). We are told to respect everyone's opinion.

That works with pizza, but not with the Constitution.

These bad habits with regard to opinion formation, type, and use are unavoidable. Whether you're an atheist (we are all human) or a Christian (we are all sinners) or anything in between, we must agree that we are all guilty, some more than others, of the behaviors described above. We cannot eliminate the tendencies of opinion, but we can be aware of them. Awareness will allow us to intercede early on our own behalf and stop ourselves from both overlaying opinions onto facts, and from confusing subjective with objective opinions. We will also be able to recognize these behaviors in others, which will let us know when a discussion is about to turn into a pointless argument. That gives us an opportunity to either try to refocus the other person, or at least walk away, which is always more beneficial than the senselessness of a shouting match over a poorly founded opinion.

THE PERSONAL ECONOMICS OF OPINIONS: INVESTMENT, SUNK COST, MARGINAL COST AND BENEFIT

So this entire communication process, were it a reality television cooking show, would come down to a reduction of a number of factors that ultimately yield a simple sauce of opinion. Even for the most learned of conversationalists, even with an unyielding emphasis on facts, that person will almost always commence their statements by saying "Well, it is my opinion that . . ." Since the formation and use of opinion is inherent in our human nature, we should not try to eliminate it or deemphasize it; instead we should embrace its reality and attempt to inform it, and in the process when appropriate, change it in ourselves and others.

An undergraduate economics major can tell you that economics is not a business discipline. Properly understood, economics is a behavioral science. Accordingly, there are principles found in economics that can help explain the problem we have with opinions, in particular with opinions held by people who wish to force facts into them instead of letting them form from facts. We have identified these concepts as problems of investment, a lack of understanding of sunk costs, and a marginal cost–marginal benefit analysis that goes on inside the opinion holder's mind, usually without their even being aware that it's happening.

First up is the concept of investment. For the typical person, they will sincerely tell you if asked that they have placed a great deal of time and energy into forming their opinions. They will share that they have read books and articles, gone to school, listened to experts, and all sorts of very wonderful-sounding things. If taken at face value, you would reflexively think that was terrific. It would be terrific if it meant that they were applying those things for each and every instance of new facts that arose. However, what they are likely saying is that they have strong opinions that they are ready at a moment's notice to fit any sort of facts (along with noise, remember). Most people, rightly or wrongly, believe they have already invested an incredible amount of time into forming soundly reasoned opinions.

What immediately follows is the fallacy of factoring in sunk costs. In economics, we are taught that when making a decision about the "next" event of any sort, it is a mistake to take into account how much money you have already spent to that point. What matters is the next dollar you spend. The money you have spent already is a sunk cost; it's gone. It is common to hear a person say something like, "I can't get rid of this car now. I just spent $1,000 on a new set of brakes. So what if it now needs another $1,000 for the transmission?" That reasoning is faulty. The brake expenditure is a sunk cost. It is gone. What matters is the cost of the new transmission versus the cost of other alternatives.

Opinions work the same way. It's difficult to get someone even to consider going through a lengthy process to potentially change opinions when they believe that they already have invested so much of their life into forming the ones they have. They have felt the same way about abortion for so many years, why would they take additional time to study some new set of facts? The time we have spent in forming opinions is a sunk cost.

There is a brilliant study that was published back in 1956 titled, "When Prophecy Fails." Three behavioral scientists were given a chance to infiltrate a Chicago-based doomsday cult whose members thought that the world was going to experience a cataclysmic disruption, caused by aliens, but they would be rescued by the aliens prior to the event. When the prophecy failed, what did many of the members do? They doubled down on their belief, created a rationalization for why the event didn't occur, and continued to believe. This study gave us the widely understood notion of cognitive dissonance we all use today. These people had simply invested too much into their belief to back away. They could not accept the sunk cost. This is, by the way, why so many people hang on to what are called conspiracy theories (actually not theories but truly hypotheses) when they do not materialize as predicted.

Marginal cost and marginal benefit analysis in economics refers to the rational approach to decision-making over what to do next. If the incremental benefit of an act is greater than the incremental cost of that act, at the margin, then it is rational for us to proceed. If the incremental, marginal cost is greater than the benefit, we should abstain. This enters into discussions over matters of opinion frequently. You will recognize it from the following statement: "You want me to look at all this information? Why? It isn't going to change my mind." When people say something like this, they are saying that the marginal cost of information acquisition is not worth the marginal benefit because their opinion just isn't going to change.

This simple modeling of economic decision-making is what is often taking place inside people who are seemingly fixated in their opinions and unwilling to openly discuss matters in a rational manner. They are forcing fact inside their preexisting opinions, and they are calculating that they have done enough investing in those opinions so that a re-examination doesn't hold positive benefit for them. There is no simple parlor trick to breaking this poorly rationalized, even subconsciously rationalized, construct. Awareness of it can provide an opening if you are able to make the strong opinion holder become cognizant of what they are doing and resultantly create a willingness inside them to change.

WHY ISSUES-BASED CONVERSATIONS GO BAD FAST

Why do issues-based conversations generally go wrong sooner and more severely than others? This is a challenging question, the answer to which I can only offer conjecture. That said, my conjecture can come from the foundation laid earlier and some of the terms and concepts we have defined.

As illustrated earlier, when people discuss fact-based issues, they are often in possession of very few facts. On some level, consciously or unconsciously, they are aware of this.

Whether it is a bad lead guitar player turning up the amplifier's volume, or a poor chef using too much spiced sauce over dried-out ribs, everybody knows that loudness and spice can at least partially cover up a lack of ability. So, when two people sit to discuss an issue, and neither one truly knows many facts upon which they can rely, they crank up the volume and the heat and they do it in a hurry. They are hoping that their demonstration of passion will distract the other party from realizing that they don't actually know (remember, facts can be known) what they are talking about.

For most people, when they are addressing a subject with which they are very knowledgeable, an almost scary sort of calm can come over them while they are discussing it with someone. So confident are they in their knowledge and expertise that they don't need to shout; they only need to inform and listen. The very best professors are like this in their classrooms. It doesn't mean they don't vary their voice for impact and theatrics; it just means they keep cool while explaining the subject matter. An experienced doctor explaining the serious nature of an illness to their patient has the same sort of calmness present in their demeanor. These people know it, and they know they know it.

If people could do a better job of understanding the above-described proper process and the impediments to informed and productive conversation, then they would be less likely to elevate their voice and their blood pressure. Knowledge breeds confidence, which leads to calm. Ignorance is the father of petulance, which leads only to pointless conflict.

SO WHAT DO WE DO NOW? (OR SHOULD WE JUST FIGHT ABOUT IT?)

The purpose of this essay has been to explain what is happening versus what should be happening before two or more people ever sit down to discuss an issue. To recap:

- We use the expression "two sides to everything," which is neither true nor relevant. There are an infinite number of "sides" based upon the number of participants. There is only one universal, finite set of facts.
- What we call "sides" are really perspectives (also points of view). Every person has one, and it is the sum total of the realities of their existence. Perspectives need to be understood and taken into account when viewing facts.
- Each person has prejudice, and it has to be understood and withheld from the consideration of facts.
- "Noise," which is the false or distracting information surrounding facts, makes it difficult to find the facts and distinguish them from the noise.
- Paraphrasing is action that takes a fact and converts it into noise by adding to, or subtracting from, the actual, original quote. Paraphrases are a very powerful form of noise.
- Analysis of facts should come from the application of a person's philosophy, ethics, and empirical knowledge. Every set of facts needs to be analyzed one set at a time.
- Opinions should be the end result of the analysis of facts. Opinions should be derivative in nature and formed only after careful consideration of the facts.
- People often approach situations with preset opinions that preclude systematic, objective analysis. They fit the facts into their opinions.
- People who apply their opinions to fact instead of deriving their opinions from fact are difficult to persuade because they are often unwilling to invest the energy into the process.

So how does this knowledge of desired process and deviation from that process help to advance civil and productive dialogue over issues?

The hope lies in the small kernel that is at the beginning of every issue, and that hope is the facts themselves. If it is possible to get a person to acknowledge the fact paradigm of fixed numbers, some known, some unknown, then you might be able to get them to consider that their opinions are being formed with at best incomplete information. This single piece of awareness could then cause them to step back, even just a little, to be more open to having productive conversation.

One issue of today that illustrates the problem better than any other is that of the current battle over man-made climate change. Nearly everyone has a strong opinion, and conversations between disagreeing parties usually take under thirty seconds to deteriorate into nothing worthwhile. But here is a question for you to consider: When was the last time you heard two people discuss climate change who were actually scientists?

Now, this is an incredibly complex issue and one that this paper has no interest in addressing, but when you place it up against the methodology previously provided, a few things are quickly apparent.

First, there are an enormous number of complex facts. Second, there is significant noise around the issue. Third, people who argue strongly tend to be from political teams and are making the arguments along the lines consistent with their political opinions; in other words, they are forcing the facts into their opinions. Very few people want to invest the time required to sort through the noise and learn all the scientific facts, nor do they have the proper education to do it even if they so desire.

I suspect that virtually everything you hear about climate change is a function of preset opinions taking in supporting noise, exercising prejudice, and firing away.

So, ask the person across from you: "What facts do you know? How do you know them? Where are they from?" Ask yourself the same questions. Compare your facts to theirs. Ask them about the perspectives they bring to the discussion. Ask them if they have any prejudices they will acknowledge and set aside. Again, ask yourself the same questions.

In the process of becoming better at asking questions, make sure you become just as good at answering them. Responding is a far more effective way to reach someone than simply declaring. Answering a question in the proper manner involves more than simply "knowing" the right answer (and remember the problem of having complete factual knowledge when you are sharing what you "know"). It is how you answer, your word choice and tone, that maximizes your answer's impact. Here is your goal in answering a question: Always convey your answer in a way that makes the listener want to ask another question.

Your own perspective can change throughout the course of your life. When viewing an event and its attendant facts, stop and ask yourself: Would I have been seeing this from the same perspective ten years ago? What has changed in my life that has changed my point of view? The answer to those two questions can help to create a heightened sense of personal awareness while engaging others.

Regarding the perspective and points of view of other people, it is worth the effort to attempt to "visit" their location whenever possible. Your perspective can never actually be that of someone else's, but if you can be a tourist to their perch, take pictures and notes while you are there. Then you can at least have some sense of how they are seeing things when you are discussing the facts of a matter. In the example shared earlier of the white accounting clerk from the rust belt and the Black clerk from Los Angeles, if each of them attempted to gain a glimpse of the other's perspective before entering conversation, a more productive outcome could be had.

We are, in the end, all human. We are inhibited and limited by our inherent faults. We cannot ever be perfect, but through a combination of humility, awareness, and vigilance, we can be better to ourselves and to others. We can be more intellectually honest with ourselves and others. Our major and very visible divisions as a nation can only be healed one conversation at a time.

Note: This entire book, including this specific chapter, is intentionally and carefully nonpartisan in nature. Of course, it should be, since it isn't about trying to advance any issue or agenda. That being said, I did use two examples involving Donald Trump. I also mentioned the *New York Times* three times and brought up the topics of abortion, Ferguson, and climate change. In none of the references was there a partisan statement. Now, ask yourself, did you leave this piece with the *opinion* that it was partisan in nature? If you did, in either direction, please go back and check what was actually written. After reviewing, did you form that opinion based upon a review of facts, or were you overlaying an existing opinion onto the essay?

Interesting question, isn't it? Take a moment to reflect here on these questions:

CHAPTER TWO REFLECTIONS

What steps will you take to change how you share ideas with others?

_____

_____

_____

_____

_____

Can you list what makes up your perspective?

_____

_____

_____

_____

_____

How about your biases?

_____

_____

_____

_____

_____

What can you do to improve how you gather and process facts?

_____

_____

_____

_____

_____

How will you check for noise?

_____

_____

_____

_____

_____

CHAPTER THREE:

AN IDEA FOR KICKING A BAD COMMUNAL HABIT

"There is no conflict of interests among men, neither in business nor in trade nor in their most personal desires—if they omit the irrational from their view of the possible, and destruction from their view of the practical."
—Ayn Rand, *Atlas Shrugged*

In May 2023, I was approached by media celebrity Melody Krell (Mel K) about collaborating with her on a book that was based upon the idea of a 12-Step recovery program. It would be designed to help Americans to start to heal from the conflict and division among ourselves.

Over a three-month period, we shared many thoughts and ideas, all of which culminated with Mel taking the work and shaping it artfully into a message that would resonate with her audience of 500,000-plus followers. Her book will become available in 2024 and I strongly urge everyone to read it when it is released.

What I have done below is to take some of the ideas that I brought to that collaboration and synthesized them into what I believe is a powerful argument that the division we are experiencing in this country today, the one I have just broken down on both the macro and micro level in the previous two chapters, is one that we have, to some extent, lost our ability to control. We have lost that ability in much the same way I lost the ability decades ago to control my intake of Jack Daniels.

In November 2016, just days after the presidential election, I was with a client discussing the upcoming Thanksgiving holiday. The client said that his large family that had celebrated Thanksgiving together for decades and through generations had just canceled their family Turkey Day dinner. Why? Because the family was so conflicted and divided over the election of Donald Trump that they felt they could not possibly break bread together. In their case, conflict wasn't going to happen at Thanksgiving because it had already happened and was irreconcilable.

That cancellation might have happened overnight, but the feelings of animosity that led to it had a longer smoldering history. While people might suddenly snap over a red wine spill on a new white carpet, the decision to cancel a long-held family tradition has a much longer fuse that's been burning. In this case, that fuse can be found in what has become a recent and virulent American addiction: *We have become a nation of conflict junkies, and we are very deep in our addiction.*

THE CUE-REWARD-RESPONSE

ADDICTION CYCLE

In my own life I have struggled against addiction, having hit bottom and "bounced" a few times before finally getting things—and myself—straight. In a real sense, everyone struggles with addiction insofar as they either have suffered from it themselves in one form or another, or they have friends or family members who have had to battle the conventional demons of alcohol, drugs, gambling, or any one of a host of habits that can make one's life "unmanageable." I now contend that Americans, writ large, have become addicted to a sort of warring with one another, which has made our lives as citizens become unmanageable.

The word "habit" here is key. Habits—sometimes good, sometimes bad—are formed within our brains from a very simple cycle: cue, reward, response. Cues, in the world of addiction, are commonly referred to as "triggers." These are things that happen in our everyday lives that lead us toward engaging in behavior that is self-destructive. As an example, for many problem drinkers, being around people with whom they have habitually partied can lead them to start to crave a drink even though they know on some level they really shouldn't have one. In our country today, our collective cue, or trigger, is evident when we encounter just about anything or anyone with whom we do not *fully* agree.

CUE

Our response to the cue or trigger is what we do typically and reflexively whenever that cue   presents itself. I find myself in the local tavern surrounded by my old sorority or fraternity members with whom I've always imbibed and so I raise a shot glass, recite an old toast, and quickly down it before even pausing a moment to consider the consequences of it (or the next twelve shots to follow). Americans are increasingly responding to disagreement, no matter how mild, by ordering a double shot of hostility with a social media chaser.

REWARD

Reward is what we think is some sort of positive we can get by responding to the cue. It is a form of satiation. What are Americans gaining from their intolerant responses to cues? It varies by person, but in general, there seems to be some sense of cathartic release and joy that comes from shouting out loud. While strong responses have their place, for the person addicted to conflict, one is too many and a thousand never enough. We are shouting at everything, and we don't need much of a cue to lead us to that point. Indeed, many Americans seem to be actively seeking out cues instead of doing what good recovering addicts do—which is to try to avoid them at all costs.

RESPONSE

Over the past decade, there have been numerous polls showing that Americans have become increasingly partisan and divided. What is interesting is that there are also polls showing that Americans are concerned over the intense polarization and division in the country. For those who are familiar with addiction, this is not at all inconsistent. Have you, or someone you know, ever uttered the phrase "I know I should stop but I just can't"? Being an addict and being an idiot are not (necessarily) the same thing. While there are many people suffering from addiction who won't admit they have a problem, there are just as many who know deep down their behavior is self-destructive, but they just don't have the means within themselves to try to quit. That is what these seemingly conflicting poll results demonstrate about everyday Americans. We know this is bad, but we just aren't ready to stop—at least, not yet.

There has been much talk about how divisive the country has become since the election of Donald Trump in 2016. The anecdote that led off this chapter has been repeated in homes all across the country with many variations on the theme. That said, polling showing concerns among Americans over the increasingly divisive nature of our engagement dates to before the Trump presidency. The simple truth is that while who is president matters, who is President isn't *all* that matters. As for Donald Trump, there is absolutely no question that his style "trumped" his substance and ideas for many Americans. I have had ardent Trump supporters say to me, "I just wish he could control himself." That said, Trump followed a president who was equally divisive: Barack Obama.

The primary difference in public perception between Trump and Obama, aside from their obvious philosophical and ideological differences, was the way that each was portrayed by the mainstream media. Trump's style was constantly hammered by reporters and pundits as being hostile and angry. Whatever one thinks of that portrayal, what is not debatable is that Obama's style, which was equally hostile to his political adversaries, did not receive the same sort of negative amplification from the legacy media. Obama's harsh statements after Ferguson, Missouri did not garner the same attention, or get the same negative spin, as did Trump's after Charlottesville, Virginia.

While it is not my contention that somehow "Obama started this," these examples are evidence that the problem is much bigger than just one man. The problem is "yuge," and the problem is ourselves.

While the polarizing personalities of Obama and Trump have contributed to our division, they have done so more by giving an excuse to be hostile than they have by actually being causative. Addicts always need to first look in the mirror. Nobody forces us to take drink, do a line, or place a bet. We are not victims; we are volunteers. How we got here is intricate and complex, but for now let's just look at where "here" is.

America has been divided before. Given the fact that we actually fought a full-fledged Civil War makes that statement axiomatic. That dramatic case isn't the only example. Other periods of time have found us seriously at odds with one another. Consider the examples of the Civil Rights Movement and the Vietnam War, to name a couple of very prominent examples. Why, then, if the country has been divided before without going to internal war and survived somehow, do we need to worry about where we are today? Won't this, too, pass? It is my belief that there is something unique about our current division and how it relates more to addiction than to differences. The distinction lies in the fact that we are now thin-slicing our disagreements in an attempt to deliberately create and express conflict.

The Civil War that erupted in 1861 was triggered over a sort of geographical dispute between Southern states (mainly agrarian and slave-owning) and Northern states (more industrial-based and slave-free) and attendant issues over states' rights, taxation, and federal authority. It was the North against the South, or Blue versus Grey. There were different uniforms and fairly clear boundaries. The North prevailed and the South, albeit slowly and reluctantly, assimilated. There was profound residual bitterness, to be sure, but eventually there was healing.

Other great dividers, such as Civil Rights and the Vietnam War, did not have clear geographical divisions but tended to be somewhat binary in nature (for or against). Some of those divisions had some demographic features to them, such as with Vietnam, you were more likely to find younger Americans protesting while older Americans were wanting to "Stem the Red tide." With the Civil Rights Movement, you were more likely to find supporters among white Americans in the North, where slavery had long been not just forgotten but rejected. Today, however, as noted above, the differences are more thin-sliced.

HOW FRIENDS BECOME CONFLICT-WIELDING FOES

Let's take the issue of abortion and two strangers who start a conversation with each other who are both "pro-life" based upon their own declared position. Now imagine these two newly acquainted folks sit down over coffee to discuss the issue. They quickly learn that they are in agreement that life begins at conception and that abortion is infanticide. Upon further discussion, one learns that the other does have a problem with forcing victims of rape or incest to carry a child to full term. The person who makes no such distinction in the murderous nature of abortion will quickly turn to saying things like, "You're not really committed. You're a plant for the other side trying to undermine our work. You can't call yourself pro-life." This can quickly lead to the other person saying, "You just want to punish innocent victims of abuse. You and I are nothing alike. I don't want to have anything to do with you." And so it goes that two people who are predominantly in agreement, on what is otherwise a very clear separation from those who call themselves pro-choice, end up attacking one another and becoming enemies.

The "cue" in this case is the disagreement over one particular aspect. The "response" is to attack and generate conflict. The "reward" is in the sense of pleasure derived from being able to tell someone else they just aren't as righteous on the issue as you are.

Addictions involve a craving for the reward. Americans are craving the reward of expressing anger and the associated adrenaline that accompanies it. What is interesting is that most Americans, if you ask them, will tell you they don't want to have conflict and they will condemn those who do. Yet they engage in the behavior anyway at almost any opportunity. They will deny it if confronted, just like an alcoholic will deny their drinking problem, but they will do it just the same. What could possibly be happening inside our hearts that leads us to behavior that we despise in others when we see it, but then turn to it ourselves almost reflexively? The answer lies not in our hearts, but in our minds; quite literally in our minds. Americans are neural-pathing in the direction of confrontation.

YOUR BRAIN ON CONFLICT

Much has been learned about the human brain over the past half-century with still much to be learned. One of the great discoveries has been that of how neural pathing works and its feature of what is called neuroplasticity. Neural pathways are a series of neurons that send signals from one part of the brain to another. At one time, it was thought that these pathways were developed only in our youth and were then sort of "set" for the remainder of our lives. Technology that has allowed for the study of brains and the mapping of activity now clearly shows that neural pathways can be altered throughout our lives. This kind of research has led to positive results for both behavioral disorders and in assisting stroke victims regain some otherwise lost capability by training the brain to do a "workaround" of a damaged area.

That ability to alter how our neurons connect has led to the concept of neural plasticity, which is just what it sounds like. It reflects the sort of "bendable" nature of the brain and how it works. Neural plasticity is what helps us to break habits by rechanneling how we respond to cues or triggers. It takes work, but the brain can be trained to blaze new trails.

That said, with anything else that offers the potential for good, bad things can happen if the mechanism is either neglected or deliberately used for nefarious purposes. Addiction is sometimes the result of a person not understanding his or her brain's ability to form new pathways. In reality, that is likely the typical case since most people don't wake up one day and say, "Gosh, I think I am really going to work on becoming addicted to something, starting today!" What can happen is that through our habitual behaviors we start to alter our pathways almost involuntarily. Our brains are a bit like water; they follow the path of least resistance. Once we start to engage in confrontational behavior, it becomes easier for our brain to follow that path, so much so that it begins to follow it naturally and subconsciously. This seems to be the case in America today. Americans have created a neural pathway in the brain that satisfies a craving. That craving, that addiction, is conflict.

Why would we do this? Why would we channel a behavior that, if you asked anyone, they would tell you they wanted to avoid? One answer to that relates to our nature as humans, something that I believe has more areas of darkness than it does of light. Another very simple answer is that we have become negligent in protecting and developing more positive neural pathways. Another answer can be found in the "state" in which many of us have found ourselves to be living over recent years. That is the state of fight-or-flight due to threats in our environment, whether real or merely perceived to be real.

AMERICANS IN FIGHT-OR-FLIGHT

From the time we are young, we learn in school about the "fight-or-flight response." This is an evolutionary concept built into us in order to protect us from sudden danger. When we are confronted with a threatening situation, a whole series of chemical and electrical impulses are sent through our brain that trigger us either to fight or to run. It is instinctive and it is designed to be a momentary burst of action designed to save us from a threat. We are not meant to stay in this state. We are supposed to use it to avoid annihilation and live to fight or flee another day. Unfortunately, in America today, many people seem to have gotten stuck in fight-or-flight mode.

Our anxiety has been building steadily, and a key contributor to it has been the presence of the internet and social media. That causative element has been with us for a while, but it has greatly expanded its power over us of late. Recent events have sent Americans on a sort of fight-or-flight "bender." Those events are: the pandemic, the George Floyd incident, and the 2020 election.

The pandemic that made its way onto American shores in early 2020 created a level of fear in people that has perhaps never really been experienced in our nation. The two World Wars in the last century cost hundreds of thousands of American lives, but those deaths occurred elsewhere and were reported back to us. In the case of the pandemic, the deaths were happening inside our homes. The 1918 Spanish flu (which likely originated here and definitely did not originate in Spain) took an estimated 675,000 American lives over a two-year period. The COVID epidemic took over a million in a shorter amount of time and was amplified by today's communication technology. While there is much disagreement over whether or not this was a treatable disease and whether or not the government used the pandemic to exploit citizens and support big pharma, one thing is not disputable: Americans were largely fearful for their own lives and those of their friends and families. Many remain fearful to this day.

When George Floyd died after an altercation with a Minneapolis police officer, the nation erupted. For some, it was a "trigger" to launch into already well-pathed conflict and confrontation preferences. Others were so outraged that they became consumed with anger and took to the streets in protests so violent and misdirected that they created their own mob mentality. Then there were those who, watching the violence, became terrified that their town, business, or home would be targeted next. Lots of fights, lots of flights.

Finally, the controversy surrounding the 2020 election and the incident on January 6th at the nation's capital served only to yet further either enflame or terrify Americans. Many were angry that their fundamental right to a fair and honest election had been stolen from them. Still others wanted to fight with those who felt that way because they saw them as unreasonable. The events of January 6th, especially the way in which they were selectively portrayed by the media and characterized by politicians, not only heightened anger, but fueled fear in those who thought that the very fundamental structure of their country was about to be overthrown.

When we say that "people can take only so much," what we are really saying is that the human brain can take only so much. Americans found themselves facing threat overload. They became stuck in fight-or-flight:

Fight went to battle.
Flight went to ground.
Reason went to the back pages of unread think tank journals.

If tendencies toward confrontation were already present within Americans prior to 2020, they certainly got triggered during that year. For those who had previously been able to engage in confrontation "responsibly," 2020 drove them into abuse. It changed their behavior. They started to neural-path differently. It wasn't entirely their fault, however. While it is necessary for the addict to take personal responsibility for their actions, the tendency or potential to become an addict makes it easier for people to exploit and take advantage of the opening.

That's exactly what has happened to Americans. If we have become addicted to confrontation, then our "dealers" have been our political leaders, media, the entertainment industry, educational institutions, and large corporations (especially their marketing departments).

AMERICA'S CONFRONTATION DEALERS

Any good drug dealer knows that if they want to sell product, they need to get the user hooked. That means they have to make the product affordable enough to realistically "score," and sometimes they might even have to give a little bit away to make sure the user has to keep coming back. That is exactly what the power structure in our country today has done. They have learned that anger and conflict keep us voting, buying, and using their stuff. When we need a fix, they provide it. This isn't new in the last few years, but it has accelerated. Powerful people, like dealers, are learning creatures. They watched as Americans became more and more addicted to confrontation, and then they realized that they could benefit from the addiction. Our addiction has helped them acquire more of the *Four P's* that come from control: power, profit, privilege, and prestige.

Those four elements have been around since the dawn of man. There is nothing new about people in positions of authority and influence using them to benefit themselves at the expense of the masses. While the objectives haven't changed, the tools available and the times in which they are applied constantly are undergoing evolution and revision. Today, technology and the anger of Americans have given these people of ill intent lots of room in which to play.

It is vital that you spend time researching and thinking about the various ways that Americans have been strung along by these dealers of division. What is important to note is that it goes back farther than just 2020. These folks have been at it for a while. There are numerous obvious examples, especially from politicians and media, some so subtle that the typical addict might miss it when trying to identify their triggers (a key part of recovery).

OUR JOURNEY—A LOOK

AT CAUSES OF EFFECTS

America wasn't always quite like this. What was the journey we took to get here, and just exactly what made us so prone to develop our addiction to confrontation? There is no question that social media has played a major role, perhaps the preeminent one. But social media didn't act alone. The bourbon can't pour itself. The addict has to participate. It is time to take a look out the window, and then into the mirror, to try and understand how we became addicted to conflict and start the process of taking responsibility for our own actions.

Our division today in America that has led us into confrontation addiction is largely the by-product of a union, a peculiar one in a sense, among three different elements:

- Powerful individuals pursuing global control.
- Academia seeking a more collectivist/communistic model of organizing society.
- Activists on the "manufacturing floor" deliberately disrupting American societal machinery to move toward socialism and collectivism.

I say this is a peculiar union because the exact goals of the three groups are not necessarily fully aligned. The first group, a global collection of people trying to gain control over the population of the globe, is not one that has any real ties to communism. They might be saying that they are heading toward a utopian future, but it is not a utopian future filled with everyone self-governing and realizing their full potential. Their utopia is one in which they, the masters of the universe, are managing our every move. They will, in their own words, replace God. Consider the following from Yuval Noah Harari, right-hand man to Klaus Schwab, head of the World Economic Forum. This is from a 2018 interview with *India Today*, but he has said variations of it on numerous occasions:

> *"So, we are in the process of becoming gods and the big question that faces us is what to do with our new god-like powers. We need ethical guidelines and goals, and nationalism cannot provide us with the necessary guidelines and goals. Nationalism thinks on the level of territorial conflicts."*

Becoming gods? Harari and his ilk are a sort of "sexual intellectual," someone so in love and attracted to their own perceived brilliance that it is almost self-seducing.

The critique of nationalism is a common theme among global leaders. They are clever in their use of terms because "nationalism" still has an association (perpetuated by the oligarchy) with the likes of Adolph Hitler and Mussolini and their fascist states of the twentieth century. While they know that condemning nationalism resonates instinctively with many people, what they really want to destroy is the nation-state. They want a world without borders, a world they can control. The most important nation-state to destroy is the United States because, owing to its many freedom-loving citizens who are in favor of individual rights, it is the most powerful in the world.

As an aside, I had an interesting revelation come to me in late 2023 while watching the film *Leave the World Behind* on Netflix. It was an embarrassing revelation insofar as it was so obvious that I was in disbelief that I had not considered it previously. There is a moment in the film when it becomes clear to one of the lead characters that the entirety of the United States infrastructure is under a comprehensive attack. He has a revelation that it isn't about some sort of star chamber of elites controlling it. Instead, it is all happening without anyone controlling it. The only thing worse than an identifiable group of rich and overeducated megalomaniacs trying to dominate the world is having the same thing happen without them.

Simply a point to ponder: What if nobody is actually in charge?

There have been many volumes written, especially in the past dozen-or-so years, that have been pointing out these global conspiracies. Unfortunately, the vast majority of people are unaware as to the full extent of what has been taking place. Their ignorance is either intentional (I don't want to know) or inadvertent (I'm too busy to look at such things). Either way, they are experiencing the effects of an ever-controlling global authority of elites, and that is making them angry. They just don't know why.

Our own government doesn't need foreigners to help us run secret programs and keep truths from the American people. Harry Truman once said that he never would have formed the CIA if he'd known it would turn into the American Gestapo. That is, of course, exactly what it has become. Despite its repeated failures as an international intelligence agency (its supposed day job), it has found the time in between promoting various forms of international *mishegas* and regime meddling.

Whether it is a modern-day global cabal of elitists flying around in private jets and being chauffeured in black SUVs with tinted glass, or people working in our own government inside laboratories or offices conducting "experiments" on us, everywhere we turn, we are being used by others to promote their own agendas.

While this is being done mostly in secret, we are feeling the effects. The results are a sort of silent killer, like a carbon monoxide leak in your home. We are choking as a people. We are frightened and we are angry.

Those with a global agenda can't take over the world on their own. They need help. As I mentioned, they are receiving it from two not necessarily unlikely, but certainly a bit coincidentally, sources: academia and activists.

In 1923, the American educational system was about to be changed forever by an event that wasn't even taking place within our country. A wealthy patron by the name of Felix Weil used his money, and Carl Grunberg used his mind, to start a new school in Frankfurt, Germany for the   purpose of accelerating the move toward communism. Marx had predicted that the movement was inevitable but that it would be driven by the forces of production—a sort of materialistic and economic approach. Weil, Grunberg, and others felt as though Marx might have been partially right, but maybe not right enough. Something needed to be done to move things along faster.

The Frankfurt School was born. It was inhabited by academics who have since become giant names in the historical field, names such as Herbert Marcuse, who eventually became the most famous member of the group when he emerged as the thought leader of the sexual and cultural revolution of the 1960s. Other members included Max Horkheimer, the group's director and a philosopher and social theorist; Theodor Adorno, a major cultural critic of the century; and Erich Fromm, who became one of the most popular writers in the United States.

In the early 1930s, with the rise of Adolph Hitler and the Nazi Party in Germany, affectations toward communist ideas became somewhat, well, inconvenient. The Frankfurt School closed up shop in Germany and eventually made its way to Columbia University in New York City, where it found a receptive home. When World War II broke out, some of its members went to Washington D.C. to contribute to the battle against fascist ideology; some went to California to explore expanded thought paths for the critical theory discipline; and some remained at Columbia.

So what exactly was the Frankfurt School of thought about? You are going to recognize it as familiar instantly. Their goal was to develop "critical theory," a comprehensive method to change society as a whole. It embraced everything from literature, to philosophy, to economics, to sociology, to psychology, and more. It drew from the work of philosophers as diverse as Georg Hegel, Marx, Friedrich Nietzsche, Sigmund Freud, and Max Weber. The Frankfurt School members synthesized philosophy and social theory to develop a critical theory of contemporary society that would combine all the abovementioned elements into a new interdisciplinary theory.

The goal? To advance us more quickly into Marx's utopian end phase of history: communist society.

If you wonder if this is where Critical Race Theory (CRT) is derived, the answer is, yes. Critical Race Theory can be thought of as a "thin slice" of critical theory, as can Critical Legal Theory, from which arose CRT. In America today, one of the most triggering concepts for confrontation is any time CRT is mentioned in schools or in the workplace. One of the problems is that most of the people fighting about it do not even know where it came from or what it really means. No matter, the term has spread, and its use has been weaponized.

The founders of the Frankfurt School would be proud. Their intention was to tear down established constructs and make way for a communist future. What the future holds is uncertain, but the tearing-down part is well underway. The influence of the Frankfurt School in American education is far more pervasive than was the COVID-19 pandemic in spreading illness. The intellectual ship that landed at Columbia in the 1930s has been churning out students and new disciples for a century. The influence is everywhere.

What is at stake is the abandonment of the traditional Natural Law/ Natural Rights principle of individual self-determination. The Frankfurt School ideas are meant to lead us along a socialist path until utopia can be reached. I am, to say the least, skeptical about utopia and very much against any compulsory move toward it So are, I believe, most Americans if they stop to think about it. The Frankfurt School, and its many derivations and academic spin-offs and inspirations, has been the single most important intellectual driver of collectivism and division of the past century. That sort of drive toward collectivism has played into the hands of the global power brokers who want us to be more reliant upon something bigger than ourselves and give that authority the power to "fix" things.

Academics, however, typically hide within hallowed halls and deliver lectures from podiums in theater-seating auditoriums. They don't usually go out and "do" anything. Turning ideas into actions requires activism, the next piece of the trilateral puzzle that has led to our division and has operated in a manner that is somewhat secretive, if not at least difficult to clearly see.

The actions of activists are divisive and troublemaking almost by definition. The goal of an activist is to upset the status quo and create change. Activism is disruptive. Martin Luther King Jr. was an activist who upset the status quo and led to reforms that increased the rights of Black citizens. Susan B. Anthony was an activist who disrupted conventional notions about women and their rights and value as members of American society. These were courageous people who placed themselves at significant personal risk— King paying with his life—in order to change the system. Their activism led to something positive.

Why, then, are we pointing to activists as part of the cause of our confrontation addiction in America today? It is because we are drawing a distinction between King, Anthony, and others like them to the kinds of activists who have operated with a darker, more sinister set of motivations. The distinction is clear and non-arbitrary. King and others worked to create change *within a system*. Other activists have been working just as hard to try and *destroy the system*.

To begin, let's return to the campus of Columbia University in New York, where in 1966, two professors in the School of Social Work, Richard Cloward and Frances Fox Piven, published an article in *The Nation* titled, "The Weight of the Poor: A Strategy to End Poverty." They wrote their piece after having been inspired by the race riots in Los Angeles. The two proposed a guaranteed annual income program and urged the Democratic party to push for it. They calculated that an enrollment push for welfare benefits would create a sort of mass collapse that could lead to a sort of socialist solution. Their strategy can best be summarized as:

- Overload the system.
- Create mass panic and hysteria as the system is overloaded.
- Oversee the destruction of the system.
- Replace the former system with a new system.

Cloward and Piven were not just creating a method for welfare reform; they were creating a paradigm that would be adopted and used time and again by radical elements in the hopes of destroying the American system. Their method has even come to be known as the "Cloward-Piven Strategy."

While Cloward and Piven made a huge contribution to the minds of those who seek to divide us, even they must bend the knee to one of the most destructive Americans (and perhaps the most destructive American) of the past 150 years. That person is the "father" of community organizing, one Saul Alinsky.

Born in 1909 in Chicago, the son of Russian-Jewish immigrants, Alinksy attended the University of Chicago, where he was taught by professors that social disorganization was the cause of poverty. By 1938, Alinsky set aside notions of a conventional professional life and entered the world of political activism. He would remain in that field until his death in 1972.

In 1971, he published his seminal work, *Rules for Radicals*. This book was a sort of guide on how to wage war against America from the inside. Alinsky wrote the following regarding what "radicals" believe:

> *The Radical believes that all peoples should have a high standard of food, housing, and health. . . . The Radical places human rights far above property rights. He is for universal, free public education and recognizes this as fundamental to the democratic way of life. . . . The Radical believes completely in real equality of opportunity for all peoples regardless of race, color, or creed. He insists on full employment for economic security but is just as insistent that man's work should not only provide economic security but also be such as to satisfy the creative desires within all men.*

That is a very collectivist, non-American, non–Natural Law view of a just society. There is no real way to reform America to get to that place. You have to tear it down. How does Alinsky propose that be done? That is where his "13 rules" come into play. In his prelude to offering those rules, he writes this about the very pragmatic Niccolò Machiavelli, the Renaissance Italian who is considered by some to be the father of political science:

What follows is for those who want to change the world from what it is to what they believe it should be. *The Prince* was written by Machiavelli for the Haves on how to hold power. *Rules for Radicals* is written for the Have-Nots on how to take it away.

Alinsky was a sort of sociopath, a man who in one paragraph talks in glowing idealistic terms, while in another he coldly and clearly discloses just how far he is willing to go. Alinsky enjoyed conflict. He has inspired generations to crave it in the same manner. The greatest trick radicals like Alinksy can ever play is to convince the world they are lovers of peace and tranquility.

Here are Alinsky's 13 *Rules for Radicals*:

1. "Power is not only what you have, but what the enemy thinks you have." Power is derived from 2 main sources—money and people. "Have-Nots" must build power from flesh and blood.
2. "Never go outside the expertise of your people." It results in confusion, fear and retreat. Feeling secure adds to the backbone of anyone.
3. "Whenever possible, go outside the expertise of the enemy." Look for ways to increase insecurity, anxiety and uncertainty.
4. "Make the enemy live up to its own book of rules." If the rule is that every letter gets a reply, send 30,000 letters. You can kill them with this because no one can possibly obey all of their own rules.
5. "Ridicule is man's most potent weapon." There is no defense. It's irrational. It's infuriating. It also works as a key pressure point to force the enemy into concessions.
6. "A good tactic is one your people enjoy." They'll keep doing it without urging and come back to do more. They're doing their thing and will even suggest better ones.
7. "A tactic that drags on too long becomes a drag." Don't become old news.
8. "Keep the pressure on. Never let up." Keep trying new things to keep the opposition off balance. As the opposition masters one approach, hit them from the flank with something new.
9. "The threat is usually more terrifying than the thing itself." Imagination and ego can dream up many more consequences than any activist.
10. "The major premise for tactics is the development of operations that will maintain a constant pressure upon the opposition." It is this unceasing pressure that results in the reactions from the opposition that are essential for the success of the campaign.

11. "If you push a negative hard enough, it will push through and become a positive." Violence from the other side can win the public to your side because the public sympathizes with the underdog.
12. "The price of a successful attack is a constructive alternative." Never let the enemy score points because you're caught without a solution to the problem.
13. "Pick the target, freeze it, personalize it, and polarize it." Cut off the support network and isolate the target from sympathy. Go after people and not institutions; people hurt faster than institutions.

Notice his use of terms like "enemy" and "target." Those enemies and targets are also known as American citizens with whom Alinsky and his disciples might disagree. Pay special attention to Rule numbers 11 and 13. These are simply monstrous.

More than any other one person and more than any other single document, this is the battle plan for collectivist and authoritarian radicals of every persuasion and subdivision. Don't think for a minute that those looking to control us haven't been feeding off the results of Alinsky's sewn divisions.

Some of you might find what has just been shared illuminating. You may have been totally unaware of these types of plots and people. To you, I say go out and research and learn more. I have only scraped the surface. Others might have their own list of those people and their organizations that have helped to tear our nation apart and who have machinated for the purpose of controlling us. Don't be offended if you think I "missed" yours.

What I have tried to do here is make a compelling argument that there are, and have been for some time, sinister forces at work trying to undermine America. While their motivations might have been different, we are at a point of convergence.

All of them have sought to divide us. It is empirically impossible to deny their success. All of them have also kept secrets. There are two ways to keep secrets. One is to hide facts and the other is to hide intentions. The people intent on fomenting division in America have been masterful at employing both as needed.

Hatred can be so blinding, it is very difficult to sometimes just shake your head, gather your thoughts, and realize that you have been played; you have been manipulated. That is what has happened to us in America. Make no mistake, we let it happen; but unlike someone addicted to drugs or alcohol who really has nobody to blame but themselves, we have been deliberately led down this path toward confrontation.

Now it will require us to be deliberate among ourselves to collectively turn around, reverse course, and try to do better.

DOING BETTER:

EVERYTHING IS PERSONAL

There is a story that circulates in Washington D.C. and beyond that has become the stuff of political legends. The story is that of the friendship and working relationship that developed between the two philosophically opposed leaders of the Republican and Democratic Parties, President Ronald Reagan and House Speaker Tip O'Neil. Google the two names together and you will get 704,000 results, most of them depicting the kinship that developed between them despite their having fundamentally opposing views on the role of government in America.

One such reference can be found in a 2013 Politico interview with former O'Neil staffer Chris Matthews, who had written a book about the relationship between the two. The article, "Chris Matthews on Tip O, Neil," reads, in part:

"There were rules in those days," Matthews said. "Tip would say, 'I'll cut a deal on Social Security if you let me focus on taxing the wealthier people.' There was always a deal. It's not that they always found common ground, it's that they each got something out of every deal. . . . A lot of times it was just getting something from the other guy. . . . There was a tremendous respect for deadlines in those days. You had to get the budget resolution in the spring, then you had to get the appropriations bill done by Oct. 1.

There wasn't this thing about brinkmanship. You had to get this stuff done. . . . There was a respect for each other and a respect for institutions." *The two also didn't suspect the worse of each other* (italics added). "Reagan was fond of Tip and completely believed that Tip wanted to help the little people. He just disagreed about how to do it."

How much of the "legend" of the relationship between these two political leaders is true can no longer be examined insofar as both of them have long since passed. For our purposes, we will simply lean on the old adage from the newspaper industry: When the legend becomes fact, print the legend!

The founder of the Common Ground Campus program, who I made clear in my acknowledgments is one of the inspirations for this book, has made the phrase "Do Better" central to its mission. It is most likely the case that you have a sense that Americans can and must do better when it comes to having civil discourse with one another. Here are some thoughts on how that can be actualized.

Let's start with one of the most commonly used, and always abused, phrases in American culture which goes, "It's not personal. It's strictly business." The fact that the phrase comes to us from Mafia lore and the *Godfather* film series ought to be warning enough as to its insidious nature. The fact that the phrase was introduced into our American lexicon only in 1972 and has become almost universally recognizable since then is a testament to its appeal; but what exactly is that appeal?

"This isn't personal . . ." is typically pulled out and used by someone when they are about to tell something to somebody that they themselves are not really comfortable saying. The employer uses it when he lays off an aging worker. The supplier uses it when he cuts off a slow-paying, but loyal and long-time customer. It is even used in variation when someone is, in fact, ending a personal relationship because of some sort of inconvenience it causes to them. "This isn't personal. I just don't have any other choice."

In short, the "This isn't personal" construct has become a rationalization tool for people to use in order to somehow detach themselves from responsibility for their actions It is a way to indicate to the recipient of uncomfortable, or even unfair, news that this just isn't their fault. There's nothing you can do. In the famous words of John Malkovich's character in *Dangerous Liaisons*, "It's beyond my control."

You can reasonably ask, "What does this communication turn-of-phrase used to rationalize behavior when getting rid of something or someone have to do with civil discourse in the private room or public square?"

The answer is that the removal of personal responsibility from our actions is habit-forming! If we can convince ourselves that the actions we take are not something for which we can be held responsible, this belief is freeing for us when we engage people on any level and in any situation. We detach our words and actions from their impact or consequence. This is a bad habit and opens us up to confrontation addiction.

What does "Doing Better" in this regard look like? *We need to realize that everything is personal! We are all persons. Walls, machinery, and organizations don't hear words or feel actions. People do. We need to be vigilant in remembering that all, not most or some, of our actions and words are personal to the recipient.*

DOING BETTER: "TOLERANCE" AND "SURRENDER" ARE NOT SYNONYMS

An absolutist will never be able to find peace in this life if they are going to demand absolute agreement from others. If we are honest, none of us can even get absolute agreement within our own selves; we simply don't choose to acknowledge that. As I have previously pointed out, in today's public discourse, if someone is part of an identifiable ideological "platoon," they immediately get criticized by other platoon members if they deviate from orthodoxy. Why on earth would somebody lash out at somebody else who agrees with them on 99 out of 100 points simply for one simple variant of opinion? That isn't rational. Addiction isn't rational. We are actually hunting for that one single point of contention so that we can kick in our addictive tendency toward confrontation. No matter how broke the alcoholic is, they can always scrape together enough coins to buy a baby pint of bottom-shelf vodka at the liquor store. The absolutist can always find that one point of disagreement so that they can purchase a shot of confrontation.

If we can recover from this addiction to confrontation, part of what we will find is that we will have a spiritual awakening as to the difference between principles and preferences. A phrase that people use quite whimsically is, "It's a matter of principle with me." The question the good skeptic needs to ask themselves when those words leave their lips is, "Is it?" Many people use the phrase so frequently, you would think them to be near righteous, but then their behavior betrays the words. They don't seem to be too terribly principled at all. What they are really saying when they state their "principle" is that they would prefer something to be a certain way. Of course, to the absolutist, there is no difference between a principle and a preference, at least to them. That lack of introspection opens them up to being susceptible to confrontation addiction.

With honesty and introspection, we can come to learn that we likely have a small handful of true principles and an enormous Alexandrian-size library filled with preferences. Those things that we merely prefer are things where we can constructively engage with others to attempt to persuade them, but not to demand that they yield. This single element alone can lower the temperature in every issue-driven room to 74 degrees with circulating fresh air.

Two simple rules of thumb to follow are these:

- *With regard to principles, hold fast while conveying them openly and honestly.*
- *With regard to preferences, be willing to adjust as might be appropriate and necessary.*

Search for the wisdom to know the difference between the two.

If that brings to mind the Serenity Prayer, then you just might have a recovery background.

What does "Doing Better" in this regard look like? *It means that we have to come to understand that tolerance and surrender are not synonyms. We can be accepting of disagreements with others because most of those disagreements relate to matters of preferences and not our rightly held principles. We will also need to surrender our quest for absolute ideological purity and full agreement on every aspect of every topic. That can best be accomplished by remembering that we don't even agree with ourselves all the time.*

DOING BETTER:

NOT ABOUT SPLITTING THE DIFFERENCE

Anyone who ever bought anything from a used car to a knock-off purse on a Manhattan street corner knows about what some call negotiating but what is really just haggling. This is where the "one previous owner" used Mustang has a sticker on it for $15,000, you offer $10,000, and the salesman says, "Let's split the difference." By meeting halfway, the buyer walks away feeling satisfied, not ever stopping to realize that the used car dealer still just made over $5,000 on the sale and likely would have gone farther down in price if the buyer had been a negotiator and not a haggler.

While professional negotiators know that "splitting the difference" or meeting in the middle is a bad tactic, regular folks view it as something that sounds fair and reasonable. Indeed, it does give the *feel* that both sides are compromising by the same amount, and if everyone had that attitude, maybe things wouldn't be so bad?

The problem is that for many people when discussing issues the "middle" is subjective and they tend to want to have the bigger piece of the remaining wishbone. How can we know what the "middle" even is in our disagreements? If there is a middle, how could we see it through all of our anger?

In an America where we are doing better, people are not focused on finding a middle. Instead, what they will focus on is understanding exactly where they are, where the other person is, and what the most reasonable place is to rendezvous that makes sense from a variety of aspects, not simply subjective distance.

I can illustrate this from my own personal experience. I have a group of thirteen high school buddies: 1980 alumni from Sault Area High School in Sault Ste. Marie, Michigan (and one an honorary member from the class of '79). We live all over the country. Each year we plan a week-long get-together somewhere. Now, one of us very good with math could find the equidistant point that would be optimal in terms of distance for everyone. The problem is that the point might be located in the middle of a quarry or a restricted government army base.

What we do instead is take into account all sorts of factors, including blackout dates for anyone, places we haven't been to before, or if one or more of the members simply would not be able to get to if it were chosen. "Not able" is a big consideration. Ultimately, our group weighs all options and chooses the best time and place for everyone. For one, it might be an hour's drive and for another it might be a cross-country plane ride. The point is that distance isn't all that matters in making the choice.

Another problem with relying on distance is that, even on their best day, people tend to overestimate the distance between themselves and others. The problem gets even more acute when they are in conflict. Said plainly, if Americans are golfers, we keep choosing the wrong club. Because we don't measure distance well, and because we tend to overestimate it, we easily get frustrated and turn to confrontation. We need a "fix." There goes meeting in the middle.

The use of social media, other than hookup sites, has made any form of finding a satisfactory meeting place all the more difficult. Engagement has become impersonal and also lacks the *need* for continuous back-and-forth. Specifically, the problem is that I can send you, or the world, any sort of nasty message and then step away from the engagement for as long as I want. Normally, this is a good thing. In business, there is an unwritten rule that when you get   angering news, you should wait twenty-four hours to respond. This helps prevent an irrational and/or damaging response. But if you are craving confrontation, the opposite can happen. It just gives more time to let anger build.

In short, social media has become anything but social and has turned into perhaps the most obvious and damaging expression of our addiction to confrontation. We need to get to a point where the users of screens can place themselves in a frame of mind that puts the person(s) with whom they are communicating right in the room physically next to them. We also need to have people realize that when they are communicating with another person on social media, they are actually communicating with the world; their addictive behavior may trigger the confrontation craving in an untold number of others.

Finally, we want to get to a place where we can "own our 1 percent" of every disagreement. Before we can bridge a divide between us and someone else, we have to be willing to acknowledge that we created at least some portion of it. When it is sincere, there are few things more powerful than someone acknowledging their role in a misunderstanding or disagreement.

As Americans, we have become increasingly less and less willing to take blame ourselves; even 1 percent. Part of "Doing Better" must include people being willing to say that what aggrieves another party isn't just a figment of their imagination. In virtually every grievance there is a bit of justification, even if it's only 1 percent of it. We all need to be willing to own our 1 percent.

What does "Doing Better" look like in this regard? *It means that we develop the right mixture of humility, awareness, empathy, and compassion to treat every encounter with others as an event that is important to us because we want it to be important to them. We must remember that it's only people who feel, who hurt, and who can engage positively and productively. There is no X (Twitter), Facebook, Instagram, or TikTok. There are only people who are using those platforms. We need to learn how to treat every individual as though they are our significant other, we love them, and they just told us they are leaving. Because in that moment, no matter who or what we normally are, we will grab their hand, look them in the eye, and say, "Wait a minute. Tell me what's wrong. I want to listen. I don't want to lose you."*

DOING BETTER: LOVE THY NEIGHBOR

While there's a well-known phrase that seems to date back to the 1400s, it became more prominent in a well-read novel of its time authored in 1896 by Charles Sheldon. That book was titled *In His Steps*, but it was the subtitle that would become famous: *What Would Jesus Do?* That phrase circulated for over 100 years before a Baptist school teacher in Holland, Michigan decided there needed to be a way to get her students to embrace the message. From that idea, WWJD bracelets were born, and for nearly a decade they could be found almost everywhere.

Jesus Christ is a figure viewed by different people in different ways. To Christians, He is the Son of God and God incarnate. To Muslims, He is a prophet. To some of the Jewish faith, He is also a prophet while still others see Him as heretical. To an atheist, He is likely seen as part of the great opiate of religion created to delude the masses. I will leave that debate to readers and theologians. Whatever you think of Jesus Christ from a religious perspective, we hope that everyone can agree that His teachings were filled with love and wisdom.

There is a passage in the Christian Bible, Matthew 22:37–39, that describes the Pharisees (the sort of leaders of the Jewish faith) trying to "trick" Jesus by asking Him a question as to which of the Ten Commandments was the greatest. Jesus confounded them with His answer, which, while translated in various ways, says this:

"Thou shalt love the Lord our God with all your heart, and with all your soul and with all your mind. This is the first Commandment, and the Second is like unto it, thou shalt love thy neighbor as thyself."

The first of those two we can respectfully set aside and let readers of all belief systems have at it (although civilly, please, and without confrontation). The second commandment Christ cites is something that Americans would be well advised to contemplate regardless of their stance on faith. We as a people have seemingly lost our way in terms of just being willing to start from the premise of loving our neighbor. In the literal sense, think of how you might react by watching the new neighbors unload their truck next door as they move in. Do you start to judge their art choices? Do you look for bumper stickers on their cars with a message with which you don't agree? Do you start to assume that their large shaggy dog is going to make a daily mess of your front yard? We have replaced "Love thy neighbor" with "Size up and judge thy neighbor."

We do this wherever we go, and while it isn't new (perhaps remember your parents telling you that the long-haired man was a hippie and he didn't bathe), what has changed is our burning desire to confront our neighbor preemptively because we are assuming that he or she is someone whom not only *might* we take issue with, but whom we *want* to take issue with! Christ wouldn't do this, and it has nothing to do with whether or not He is God. It has to do with something that our grandparents taught us. It has to do with simply being decent.

As I always like to say, and mention elsewhere in this book, you can make an argument that the two most impactful people in all of history, one on the secular side and one on the religious, were Socrates and Jesus Christ.

They share two things in common. The first is they were both forced to give their lives for their teachings. The second is that they both changed the world not by arguing with others in heated exchanges, but by asking them questions.

The best way to get someone to see *your* point of view is to have them voluntarily come to form it as their *own* point of view. The religious might call this a conversion. Conversions come through contemplation, revelation, and self-awareness. This can best be generated by asking questions of others and by letting them hear their own answers. You don't talk them into something; they end up *talking themselves* into it. There is no greater evidence of conversion than to have someone with whom you are talking to tilt their head, scratch their chin, and say, "I never thought of that."

Another interesting thing about "conversions" is that they only stick if they are voluntary. You can shout someone into submission but not into lasting agreement. Even little nuances in our conversations can make a huge difference. Consider choosing the phrase "I think you're wrong" versus saying "I see it differently." The former leads to confrontation while the latter leads to open listening and contemplation.

Socrates knew that. Jesus knew that. They asked questions and they changed the world. If you start by loving your neighbor, if you start by asking, "What would Jesus do," it gets much easier to engage them with an open mind and start to have an open question-and-answer conversation. Who knows? You might even get a conversion!

What does "Doing Better" in this area mean? *It means that Americans will become more willing to live Martin Luther King Jr.'s words of judging people by the content of their character and not anything else. It means taking the time to learn and understand what is inside each person and where they come from and why they believe what they believe. It means asking questions. It means keeping four simple letters in mind: WWJD?*

When Sir Thomas More penned *Utopia* in 1516 about this sort of idyllic place of cooperation, it was lost on many that the word "Utopia" comes from the Greek and means "nowhere." Perfect places, like perfect people, simply don't exist.

I learned in recovery that perfection is not a goal of the process. People in recovery simply start from the premise that their lives have become unmanageable owing to their addiction. A common phrase we use is, "Together we do get better." There isn't a person who has successfully worked a program for thirty years and remained sober who would tell you that their life is perfect. What they likely will say is that their life has gotten better and it is no longer unmanageable.

If we were seeking perfection in our interactions with one another, that would make us a sort of absolutist, and I have made clear that the absolutist will face no happiness in this life (perhaps in the next). What we do seek, what is reasonable to seek, is that we make our lives with one another manageable again, no matter our differences.

Another phrase I learned in recovery is, "It works if you work it and sucks if you don't." Right now, what we are doing in our country sucks. What we are experiencing is not sustainable. We keep throwing insults into the canyon and the echo keeps throwing them back. There is another phrase we use to warn people about the risks of not getting sober. We say that what awaits them is, "jails, institutions, and death." Take that idea as you might with regard to the need for all of us to do better in ending our constant conflict. I'm hoping that what I have shared in this chapter, and what I share throughout this book, can help contribute to building some honesty, open-mindedness, and willingness in all Americans. Just like my sponsor told me when I first started working a program, **what you do with it is up to you.**

It truly is possible to recover. In the summer of 2022, I went through an approximate 45-day period that carried with it a great sense of personal sadness and loss. There were days when I would sit down to write (I was in the finishing chapters of the book I coauthored with the late Dr. Vladimir Zelenko), open my laptop computer, stare at the screen for a few minutes, and then close it back up and spend the day lying on my sofa unable to do much of anything. I ultimately managed to finish that book and deliver it on schedule. I did so, according to what I have been told, and that reviews online confirm, at a very high-quality level. To this day, I have no idea how I did it.

That isn't the only thing that surprised me. About thirty days into my journey of darkness, it occurred to me that I hadn't even thought about having a drink. Imagine that my first thought of alcohol was one in which I realized I hadn't thought of alcohol. I was experiencing great personal pain, and I was doing it without even considering dosing with my old faithful medication. The habit, you see, had been broken.

My dear readers, I suggest to you that if I made it through the summer of '22 sober, you can find a way to make it through a day, then a week, then a month, then who knows without giving in to the temptation of confrontation. I assure you there is a better way.

REFLECTIONS FOR CHAPTER THREE:

Take an inventory of yourself and see where you are guilty of slipping into confrontation.

_____

_____

_____

_____

_____

List five ways you can and will do better.

_____

_____

_____

_____

_____

Think of someone you might gave recently been too aggressive with either in person or social media. Make amends to them.

_____

_____

_____

_____

_____

CHAPTER FOUR:

AN IDEA ABOUT DISSIDENTLY SPEAKING

"Most people do not really want freedom, because freedom involves
responsibility, and most people are frightened of responsibility."
—Sigmund Freud, *Civilization and Its Discontents*

This is not an essay[3] I intended to include in this book. Then as I finished revising Chapter 1, the original "How America Broke Its Wings," and as I contemplated the courageous actions of four students at Hope College in Michigan in the fall of 2023, I changed my mind.

I was set to visit Hope College on November 14, 2023 with the "Common Ground Campus (CGC)" program, which was started by my brilliant and visionary partner Felisa Blazek and myself. One of CGC's programs, *Bridge to Tomorrow*, is designed to put students from both sides of some divisive campus issue onstage in front of their peers. Instead of debating the issue, CGC tries to have these students find ways to come together and solve problems. The topic for Hope College was set to take on concerns under the heading of "Diversity, Equity, and Inclusion."

With just over a week to go, we had four bright and differing students set to participate and had support both on campus and in the community. Then something happened. A professor stepped in to try and stop the event. Because my partner's and my personal politics were associated with Team Right positions, he did not want us on campus or the program to take place.

Incredible pressure was brought to bear on the students to withdraw and the college to cancel. It didn't work. The college president did not withdraw approval, and the students, facing extraordinary peer and academic pressure, stayed with the commitment. The event was a great success. Each of our four

---

3   Originally published as: "Understanding and Embracing the Role of the 21st-Century American Dissident," 2021; revised, 2022

students shared concerns they had over particular DEI-related issues, and we were able to find ways to address those concerns that all the participants could accept. We found common ground.

After the event, we sat with the student participants and enjoyed beverages and conversation. I especially enjoyed the dialogue with the students who would be associated with Team Left. These are brilliant young people; articulate and informed. Perhaps we did not see solutions in the same way, but we shared an openness and willingness to engage civilly and in a stimulating manner.

We shared something else. None of us at the table wanted to live under an oppressive, totalitarian state.

The people we call "leftists" or "liberals" in this country are too often associated with those who want to oppress us. That happens because they are generally more willing to use government and public policy to solve problems than are those labeled as "right-wing" or "conservatives." This is a tragic mistake. They want to be free just as much as anyone else; they just have different ideas as to how to use their freedom and how to share it with others.

So, I offer this piece with Jonah, Marlie, Shane, and Therese in mind. I don't want any of you to fall under the shadow of a despot. I want us all to remain free to be able to discuss our differences and solve problems together peacefully . . . spiritedly, but peacefully and under an umbrella of freedom. Thanks to each of you for opening my eyes and changing my life.

WE HAVE TRAVELED FAR

(IN THE WRONG DIRECTION)

For those who value Constitutional ideals and individual liberty, the past few years have been a fresh form of hell. Beginning with the lockdowns leading into the *mishigas* surrounding the 2020 election, and then transitioning rapidly into the taking of political prisoners, vaccination mandates, and the imposition of aggressive socialist policies, we have watched the ravages of collectivism sweep across our nation like a California wildfire. Who could have imagined such a deterioration taking place in American life so quickly?

We should not be surprised. If you chart the path on which our nation has been traveling for a very long time, and if you understand that we do not live in a world of cycles or swinging pendulums, everything makes sense. We live in a world of cause and effect, trajectory, and velocity. Applying that to the 2022 midterms, the United States has been traveling along a path toward obliterating the structures our Founders put in place for well over a century. This has been evidenced by various strands of cause-and-effect events and policies that have been converging to a central point. Like wiring that runs through your home with each originating in separate rooms, collectivist runs have now finally come together at our societal circuit panel, reaching a critical unified mass.

What's more, the events of the past couple of years have led to this collectivist, totalitarian juggernaut gathering speed. Force equals mass times acceleration. Strands of collectivism have joined together, and they have accelerated. There is tremendous force. You don't stop that and reverse it during some silly midterm election cycle.

The reason the last few years of national misery under a fascist model of socialism didn't create some overwhelming backlash at the polls is so obvious that it's easy to miss.

The last few years didn't create a backlash because they were a natural consequence of over 100-plus years of choices. The nation brought itself voluntarily to this point. Why would it all of a sudden decide to start over?

Those of us who don't like what we are seeing in America need to understand that we are not in a position to change it quickly because we have been reduced to becoming dissidents. We are people who on paper have the same rights as everyone else but who, in reality, do not get to have those rights functionally. We are suppressed, we are silenced, we are arrested. Sound familiar? It is what we saw in Eastern Europe in the last half of the last century, and what we continue to see elsewhere in the world. It is what I wrote about and warned about in January 2021.

It is my hope that within the darkness of these pages, you will find light. We are not the first people to have lived under the boot of totalitarianism. Others have and others have found a way to triumph. The good news for us is that right now that boot's press upon our throat is still relatively light. The bad news is found in its potential to press more forcefully at any moment.

We must play the long game to reverse this process. Whether we like it or not, we're all inside the game; it's best we start actively playing. All that's required is strength, smarts, perseverance, and above all, patience.

Please enjoy this new version of an internationally read piece. It is my understanding that it has been used in a reader group's "club choice" in Australia, a "member's guide" in a British Columbia's political organization, and an operation manual for a citizens' activist group in Colorado. When I originally penned it, I never could have imagined its impact.

JANUARY 19, 2021 (AND REVISED)

In the early days of 2021, two stories were circulating that most people would not necessarily associate with one another. In Russia, opposition leader Alexei Navalny[4] returned to Moscow after having spent several months in Germany recovering from an attempt on his life by means of the old Soviet method of poisoning. In what was almost certainly at the direction of Vladimir Putin, Navalny was arrested as he stepped off the plane.

Meanwhile, here in the United States, Russia's opponent during the Cold War, the City of Philadelphia took the gun away from 51-year-old Police Detective Jennifer Gugger.[5] Her "crime"? She attended the rally in Washington on January 6th. There was no indication that she was inside the Capitol; she was simply at the rally. She posted some strong statements on social media, especially about Vice President Mike Pence, but not anything that would constitute a direct threat.

What do these two seemingly quite different people have in common? They are both dissidents. They both acted as though they had the right to say and do what they said and did. They were both mistaken. In Russia,

---

4   https://www.nytimes.com/2021/01/17/world/europe/navalny-russia-return.html

5   https://www.inquirer.com/news/jennifer-gugger-gun-taken-capitol-trump-pence-20210112.html

given its history of totalitarianism, Navalny likely knew what he was getting himself into. In our country, however, where totalitarianism is in its infant stages, it is quite likely that Gugger was caught unaware.

This is going to be commonplace for many of us over the next several years as we are forced to come to grips with the fact that this is no longer the "land of the free and the home of the brave." We can stomp our feet and deny it, we can try to act as though we don't accept it, but it is not going to change the reality that the great American experiment that was launched just over 230 years ago is finally producing empirical results. The conclusion? *People are capable of sustaining individual liberty only for as long as they can be constrained by a system of law that suppresses and contains their true nature.*

Hobbes was right.

For those of us who still believe in and embrace the ideas of our founding, for those who believe that the individual and their liberty are of paramount importance and prime value, for those of us who believe that free market capitalism is the most moral and just system for organizing economic activity, we need to have an epiphany. We need to awaken to the reality that we are not a majority. We are not a vocal minority with the same rights as the majority. We are now dissidents. We do not have the same voice as our ever-strengthening oppressors, and we do not have the same rights that they enjoy.

For those who might argue that there are more of us, or at least as many of us, who believe in individual liberty and free market capitalism than there are opponents to the same, I would suggest that you should not confuse a simple head count with total political atomic mass. The positions within society that our opponents hold and the institutions and machinery they control give them leverage beyond simple membership numbers.

As to our being cast in the role of dissidents, we have no choice. How we conduct ourselves in that role will be the difference between having a chance over the long term to ultimately prevail, or having to spend a century or more under a totalitarian thumb. We need to understand the role we are in, the most effective course of action we can take, and above all, we must understand and accept our limitations. A failure to understand and accept the latter will only deepen and prolong our subjugation.

THIS IS NOT ABOUT AN ELECTION

Understandably, there has been a great deal of focus on the events that have happened since November 3, 2020. Probably half the country feels as though the reelection of President Trump was stolen through some combination of Chinese interference, voting machine manufacturers, corrupt state and local election officials, and overzealous volunteers. I address that issue in a separate essay, which follows this one. This treatise is not about that. In fact, there is a way in which the election of November 2020 was completely irrelevant in terms of what has happened to transform the United States.

There is a myth that political events happen in cycles or that there is some sort of swinging political pendulum that goes too far one way and then overcorrects to the other. People make this mistake because they confuse election results and prevailing political parties with directional changes for the nation. While it is true that election results can swing from cycle to cycle, and while there has been a historical back-and-forth regarding the occupant of the White House, the actual direction of the country in terms of diminishing individual liberty has been consistent over the past one hundred years.

Said mathematically, if the x-axis is time and the y-axis represents level of liberty (with a baseline set in the late 1780s when our nation launched), we have been steadily descending toward the x-axis for a very long time. We are now about to test the limit function we learned about in calculus class.

In less than twelve months, we hit three inflection points along that downward-sloping line that have led to its descent at an ever-increasing rate. The first was the advent of the pandemic, which made people susceptible to government control and allowed governments to gain control. It also instilled in us the willingness to and even reveling in turning in one's neighbor.

The second was the incident involving George Floyd, which tapped into an individual's notion of shame and triggered a societally conditioned need for self-sacrifice (altruism). Millions of people came to feel that they somehow had to surrender something, anything, to right a social wrong that was identified with catchphrases such as "social justice," "police brutality," and "black lives matter."

The third inflection point was the rally in Washington D.C. on January 6th, which provided a visual image that could justify having to silence our speech, remove us from our positions, and generally limit our freedom in order to "protect us from unruly and dangerous elements."

Over a period of less than twelve months, the American "body politik" was given a mainline injection of an emotional cocktail that included fear, shame, guilt, dependency, revenge, anger, class struggle, oppression, and even empowerment (for those joining the "cause"). We created what conservative commentator Charlie Kirk calls "micro tyrants," people of normally limited status who by virtue of their position were able to exercise authority over others (wear your mask, keep your distance, and so on). These were people used to feelings of limited significance who were suddenly given the ability to be part of something bigger. Something that was moving. Something that had force.

Of all the factors, fear has probably been the primary driver. Politicians and the media have stoked the public's fear masterfully. Fear of the Chinese coronavirus, fear of riots, fear of insurrection, fear of their neighbor, fear of just about everything. Fear is what triggers the basic fight-or-flight response in humans. During a crisis, that instinct can save our lives. Living in fear for a protracted period of time, however, can destroy our psyches and take away nearly everything that makes us a rational, skeptical being. (Dr. Mark McDonald, who became the "Dissident MD" subsequent to this original piece, has written brilliantly on this subject.)

We made playing "victim" a status—a sought-for attribute often contrived, which has been gaining membership and momentum for over thirty years—something that brought with it not only an entitlement to get from others, but now an entitlement to outright take from them. At the heart of this is, as it has been for millennia, the attack on private property. You have too much. You acquired it unjustly. You exploited others in the process of acquiring it. These arguments are as old as man himself, but they have taken on a new sort of tone in twenty-first-century America.

We also created a new way for humans to group together and exploit other humans through what Victor Davis Hanson has termed the "Zoom/ Skype Class" and the "Muscular Class." This conflict is between the people who got to sit at home in comfort during the Chinese coronavirus and the real men and women out there who were doing the work that needed to be done to keep the country fed, warmed, cooled, etc. This has led to a feeling of empowerment on the part of the Zoom/Skype Class over those in the Muscular Class and feeds the inclination to control and subject.

All of these seemingly disparate elements have one unifying theme: They are all hostile to individual liberty and free market capitalism. The hostility to these twin towers of American exceptionalism was present and steadily increasing over the course of several generations. All recent events have hastened their receding into the shadows and their being replaced by groups of people wanting to make collective decisions for all, and with a group of citizens receptive to having them make those decisions.

That leaves those of us who still believe both in the ideas of individual liberty, which are codified in our Constitution, and in the virtue of free market capitalism as threats to the new order that has been forming.

That makes us dissidents.

For anyone who holds to the notion that if only Donald Trump had won the election, none of this would be happening, check your premises. Look what happened in this country over the four years while Donald Trump was president! This is much bigger than one man or any one party. This is historical in nature and involves over 200 years of continuous cause and effect.

People who are learned in history like to point out that our Founding Fathers were inspired by the likes of Aristotle, John Locke, Montesquieu, and Adam Smith. These were all great thinkers whose ideas, when joined together, led our Founders to design a country that would enable the freedom of man, freedom they felt was man's natural state, to take hold in virtually every aspect of their daily lives. It is fair to say that, without these philosophers, America might have existed, but it would not have existed as designed to promote so much individual freedom. To promote the best hopes for man.

Regarding that design, there was another element. It is true that our Founders took their inspiration from the great Natural Law thinkers of the Enlightenment. It is just as true that they had read that most foreboding of pre-Enlightenment thinkers: the Englishman Thomas Hobbes. Hobbes, who wrote his seminal piece, *Leviathan,* in the early seventeenth century, warned of man's true nature, that of a fearful moral relativist who was incapable of living civilly without the oversight of a strong monarch.

Our Founders wanted nothing to do with a strong monarch, but they took Hobbes seriously. They built such a complex system of government with so many fail-safes to protect us from ourselves that they hoped it would be able to contain our nature.

However, give a madman locked in a stone-walled room a heavy-duty spoon and enough time and he will find a way to dig through the walls. After 200-plus years, human nature in America has escaped its Constitutional walls. There are many of us who want to put the beast back inside.

We are now called dissidents.

WHAT IS THE SOCIETAL STRUCTURE

FACING A DISSIDENT?

Not every society that has experienced the various forms of despotism has faced the same internal structure. America's movement toward a totalitarian state is unique (some Western European countries have similarities but not enough to be considered parallels) because of its having so recently occupied the position of being the world's leading country in terms of both individual rights and free market capitalism. The structure we find ourselves in now is a function of the structure that we built and are now leaving.

Consider the series of concentric circles shown below. They represent our current American situation. The placement of these circles is not going to change for quite some time. The only alteration will be seen in their relative size and in their increasing "rigidness."

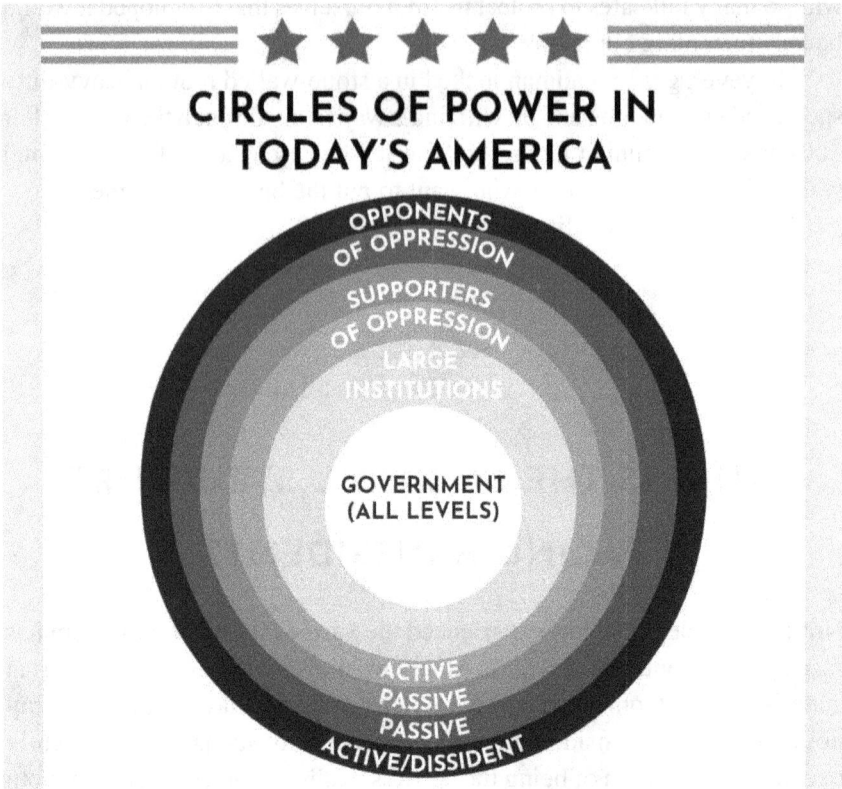

At the core, we have the government. It is the government, and only the government, that has the power both to set actual law and to enforce the law through criminal penalty. That places them at the power center. However, in today's America, it is only their enforcement capability that earns them that spot. In today's America, the second circle, that of institutions, is the one truly steering the government and setting its goals and objectives for managing the lives of others.

The circle of large institutional partners are those players who are both large enough and wealthy enough to guarantee their influence. They are also players where their leaders (board members, C-suite members, public faces, etc.) are united in the desire to suppress both individual liberty and free market capitalism (more on that seeming contradiction later).

Members of this institutional circle, which if drawn to scale would be quite large, include:

- Big tech companies
- Other large publicly traded companies, especially commercial banks

- Primary and secondary education units
- Colleges and universities
- Large media organizations
- The entertainment industry

These institutional groups are playing a significant role in reducing freedom. There is nothing about this that is new, just accelerated. For example, the attack on individuals versus the collective and the assault on capitalism on college campuses has been underway since the 1960s. The media's hostility to the same ideas lagged behind universities as the educational system that produced them needed them to enter the workforce and take control of the various corporate and institutional cultures. This is true of other large companies and institutions, as well.

In the next circle are citizens, acting in their capacity as individuals outside of whatever occupation they might have, who generally support the oppression of individual liberty and free markets. This group can be broken down into two subgroups:

- Those who actively and knowingly support
- Those who passively, perhaps unwittingly, support

The distinction matters with regard to the activities of dissidents. While it is not possible to know the exact percentage breakdown of the two subgroups, it is important to realize that the dissident focus needs to be on members who are passively, even unwittingly, supporting the oppression.

Finally, in the outer circle, we have those who stand squarely in support of individual liberty and free markets. Like the circle inside it, the members of this group can be broken down into two subgroups:

- Those who are passive in their support (inner ring of last circle)
- Those who are active in their support (farthest away from core)

You can see that those who are opposed to tyranny are in these outermost circles and the farthest removed from the power structure.

It is vital for these two outermost groups that they do not further fracture. Given their status as outsiders, membership is critical. This means that those who are "active" in their dissent cannot become critical of those who are passive. To do so risks their alienation and could push them into the circle below. We need to understand that not everyone has the same tolerance for risk. Nor everyone has a set of life circumstances that enables them to actively join a dissident movement. For those of us who can join, we must join on behalf of the others. We are already so far removed from the powerful core that we cannot risk alienating anyone who stands behind us, even if circumstances prevent them from standing alongside us.

Two points of clarification are needed about this model. The first is with regard to the inner circles that include governments and institutions. It must be noted that we exist under a bell curve. It is not the case that all governmental units will participate in all forms of suppression at equal levels, or even at all. For example, the citizen living in Florida will experience a much higher level of individual liberty and ability to engage in local commerce than will the resident of Illinois.

What I contend is that at the mean and out toward two or three standard deviations, governmental units of all types will become increasingly assertive in limiting individual liberty and free market capitalism. Enjoy the havens that are ten standard deviations away from the mean and consider outliers to be the equivalent of winning the freedom mega-lottery.

The other point in need of addressing is that the individuals in the third and the fourth circles are also often members of the inner two circles when it comes to employment. This is not an inconsistency, but rather points to a structural design flaw in the inner two circles and creates one of the opportunities for the ultimate victory of dissidents. There is no actual living organism that is named government, nor are there any that can be called institutions. Both are nothing more than compositions of individuals; individuals who live in those two circles farthest from the power structure, but who are involved, in fact running, those power structures as part of their normal lives.

In their day jobs, people of both the outermost circles come together in the workplace to interact. Those who are supportive will be more likely to embrace the suppressive activities of their employers. Those in the outer circle will be less so. The daily interaction in the workplace (classroom, congregation, coffee shop, etc.) will provide an opportunity for the properly acting dissident, over time, to cause their oppression-supporting coworker to start to question themselves. It will lead them to check their own premises. Having the supporters of suppression, especially the ones who are passively or unwittingly supporting it, see the targeting of dissidents for punishment can ultimately lead to their making the most powerful statement that any citizen can possibly make on behalf of another:

Hey, that doesn't seem right.

This is the new social stratification in America, and the dissident lies at the outermost ring, removed almost completely from the center of power. It is critical for the dissident to understand their position vis-à-vis others in order to understand how to penetrate and dismantle their opposition. Failure to do so will lead to self-destructive behavior. Mistakes will be made in assuming they have more power than is actually possessed.

We cannot assume that we alone can cause the system to collapse or accommodate. We are the outer ring. We need help. We need to be able to get at the system and eat at it from the inside out. That means turning our cherished notions of individual liberty and free market capitalism into a sort of American virus that can lodge within the totalitarian framework, multiply, break it down, weaken it, and kill it. We must work within the system to break the system. That is what dissidents do.

Regarding the "system," one of the biggest mistakes that is going to be made by dissident Americans relates to their assumption about "rights."

BY WHAT RIGHT . . .

Americans are big on individual rights. Our Declaration of Independence starts out with referencing our "inalienable rights." The first ten amendments to the Constitution are called the "Bill of Rights." It is these rights that those in support of individual liberty and free market capitalism seek to defend and preserve. These are the rights that virtually all Americans believe they possess. They must possess them. The Constitution says so. To be very literal, "inalienable" means "unable to be taken away from, or given away by, the possessor."

This is where the dissident needs to discern the difference between the "is" and the "ought." It is black-letter clear that each and every American ought to have the same rights as every other American. Unfortunately, that is not the case. When those in control of government decide that they will not apply the laws in the same manner to all people, then some people effectively no longer have the same rights. They may retain them theoretically, but functionally those rights are gone.

We all know that, at a crosswalk, cars are required to stop for pedestrians. We also know that if we begin to step into a crosswalk in front of a car approaching at what seems to be about three times the permitted rate of speed, we will be killed for exercising our "right" to cross the street at that place and at that moment. This is the example that the effective dissident needs to bear in mind.

Americans often speak of "natural rights" or "rights given to us by God." These ideas seem consistent with the "inalienable rights" mentioned in the Declaration and seem to be codified in the Bill of Rights. While most people make mention of them, few understand their actual derivations.

Natural rights are derived from what we call "Natural Law." There are really two categories of Natural Law theory, neither truly conflicting with the other, but also not identical. One could be the more religion-centered version held by Thomas Aquinas or William Blackstone, that there is a natural law set forth by God and that all people are capable of understanding it through their own reason and God's grace and revelation.

The other concept is more secular in its formation and is the sort held by John Locke or Montesquieu, that Natural Law is in accordance with the laws of nature and that man's right to be "free" is as fundamental as is any other rule of order found in nature. Most Americans don't know that "life, liberty, and the pursuit of happiness" are an intellectual direct lift from Locke's "life, liberty, and property." You don't have to believe in an unmoved mover to believe in a natural law (but it probably helps).

Either way, Americans have come to believe, rightly so, that their absolute rights to "life, liberty, and the pursuit of happiness" are not to be afforded to them by the government. Government's role is to protect those rights, not to grant them.

While that argument may be theoretically sound and morally right, it is not a reflection of reality. While we may all possess those rights innately, we do not possess them functionally if the government decides to take them away. Did the citizens of Eastern Europe under the Soviets not have natural rights? Do the people of Cuba not have natural rights? Do the people of China not have natural rights? Regarding the possession of natural rights, if one does, all must. Yet we see the people of those times and places denied access to their natural rights. Rights are only as real as the power structure that enforces them recognizes their existence.

The new American dissident needs to understand that they will be denied access to them, as well. Failure to acknowledge this reality will cause the American dissident to be needlessly struck down, either literally or figuratively, and removed from the dissident movement. We will have martyrs, but we do not need an assembly-line-style production of them. We need to learn to say, "I used to have the same rights as you," not "I have the same rights as you."

Already we are seeing the beginnings of this with incidents like the police detective mentioned at the beginning of this piece having her service pistol confiscated while her political activities are being reviewed. We have people who have lost their jobs, effectively facing discriminatory practices in the workplace, for their political views. We have students losing scholarships. This list is long and it is growing. Anyone who denies that reality places themselves and those around them at risk. (As of the date of this revision, we have political prisoners locked away in the D.C. jails for simply trespassing on January 6th. This would have been unimaginable until very recently)

This is not a call to pacifism. On the contrary. It is a call to reality. To be a dissident means to do the work that you can do, placing yourself at risk, while working around the easy ways to snuff out your efforts. Posting a dissident piece of content on Facebook will simply have you removed from Facebook and without redress. We need to find paths of least resistance in which to undertake our activities.

One of the key things to keep in mind is that those who occupy the circle just underneath ours, the people who are supportive of the oppression, will have more rights than we have, but only so long as they remain supportive. They are only a single statement, action, or "post" away from joining us in the outer circle. Some are aware of this so they will be hesitant to express their support. Some are not aware and will be shocked and frightened when their rights are suddenly curtailed, causing them to want to move back to their prior circle. As dissidents, we need to be aware of the problems facing those who decide to join us. We need them prepared for what they will face. We need to try to instill courage in others while mitigating shock. This will help us not only to convert new members to our side, but to make those conversions take hold.

Above all, we have to accept that we no longer have access to those rights given to us by God or by nature. Our fight is to recapture them, not to throw a petulant fit and insist we still have them.

An effective dissident knows this.

RULES FOR BECOMING
AN EFFECTIVE DISSIDENT

What exactly should we do in our role as dissidents? That's a great question and leads to the first, and golden, rule for becoming a dissident in today's America.

WHAT'S THE "GOLDEN RULE"?
GREAT QUESTION!

Let's break Western Civilization into two segments, secular and religious, and ask this question: Who was the most important dissident in history? In each segment, I believe we can come up with a clear winner: Socrates and Jesus Christ, respectively.

Socrates planted a flag in the ground for reason and rational thought. He built his intellectual "church" upon the rock of Plato, the philosopher to whom other philosophers say all must answer. Every advancement in Western Civilization, whether in agreement or not with the Ancient Greeks, is somehow derivative of what Socrates started.

As for Jesus Christ, there is hardly a need to defend this choice. To the extent that Judaism preceded Him and launched Him, He transcended it. As for other religions of the world that already existed, He surpassed them. As for religions that came after, they were in answer to Him. He built His church upon the rock that was Peter, and the world has never been the same.

These two great dissidents had two things in common. First, they were both killed, dramatically and tragically, as thanks for their efforts. Second, and more lastingly, they both embraced a method of teaching that caused them to last eternally and grow in influence:

They asked questions.

It is important to remember that while the two innermost sections of the new social structure are government and large institutions, neither of these are thinking things. They are merely vessels that are controlled and occupied by thinking things, also known as humans. We cannot reach "government" and we cannot reach "Facebook," but we can reach the humans who are in control of the machinery. We cannot lose track of this. The moment we make the enemy nameless and faceless and nothing more than an abstract representation, then we can no longer reach it in any way, and it cannot be defeated.

The role of a dissident is not to convert those who are already on their side. The role of a dissident is to convert those who are opposed but who eventually come to realize and accept the teachings of the dissident. This comes through self-revelation. Self-revelation is created through awareness. Self-awareness is best created by posing a question to the listener that causes them to tip their head, scratch their chin, and say to themselves, "I never thought of it that way."

We will not be able to win this war in which we now find ourselves by fighting. We can win it only through persuasion. We need to teach. We need to lead by example. We need to ask questions, especially to the power structure and in front of the circles beneath us. This ought not to seem daunting or overly complex. Each and every one of us will be up to the task.

That is because these questions will come in two very fundamental forms: Why, and why not?

When we ask those questions of the government, of academia, of industry, of the news media, we already know the answers they will give. For your safety. For the greater good. To protect others. And so on. We don't need to hear the answers and the explanations; others do. Over time, the sheer weight of those answers will start to ring hollow to the supporters of oppression.

We all know how silly someone looks when they are asked a simple, direct question and seem to be unable or unwilling to answer it. When we make them do so in front of others, those who are listening start to take notice.

One last note regarding the golden rule of being a dissident and it is going to be uncomfortable. Not only do you have to be willing to ask questions, you need to be willing to answer them when asked. Assume the person asking you to defend your position is sincere. They may not be, but in assuming they are, you will provide a thoughtful answer, one that might just resonate with those around them.

OTHER RULES AND SUGGESTIONS FOR EFFECTIVE DISSIDENT ACTIONS

We can't show we are being persecuted if we continue to capitulate. Anyone who wants to join in the effort to restore individual liberty ought to be able to find something in the following list that fits with their skills, or talents, or passions, or some combination of the three. All you need then is willingness.

If you can't do everything, do one thing. This might be the most important of all the suggestions. I had many people approach me over the past couple years who have expressed frustration about the path the country was on who also lamented their inability to be more active in "the fight" because of their life obligations. Everyone can be active because everyone can find at least one form of dissident activity to which they can join. Do some basic math. Assume there are 330 million people in this country. Then assume that half of them (165 million) are in one of the two outer rings. Finally, assume that every one of those 165 million engage in at least one form of dissident activity. Eventually there will be that straw that breaks the totalitarian back. You could be that straw.

Take back our language. Nowhere have we voluntarily surrendered more ground to the collectivist horde than in the area of language. From their ridiculous use of pronouns to their renaming of sports franchises to their alteration of holidays, those who want to control us know that the best way to start is by defining the words we use and to tell us when we are allowed to use them. When we let this happen, we are engaging in self-censorship. This is where political correctness started and where cancel culture has picked up.

We have to show enough courage to at least start using words the way they are defined and the way in which they were intended to be used. This alteration and corruption of language is right out of the Critical Theory playbook developed by the Frankfurt School, and it is only as effective insofar as we surrender to its demands. Stop surrendering.

Make those complicit in our oppression feel the hurt of a severed relationship. We all have the "friend" who goes on social media and posts something like, "All conservatives are fascists." They talk about people who believe in individual liberty and free market capitalism as the proverbial "they," "them," and "those" people. We might then approach that friend and remind them that we are conservative. What does the friend say? Almost always the answer is, "Oh, I didn't mean you. You aren't like the others."

When this happens, we need to learn to say to them, "Yes, I am like the others, and you have the others wrong. When you insult them, you insult me. Goodbye."

I use "conservative" as the example, but the same can apply to "liberal." As those four courageous students at Hope College taught me, they don't want to become serfs either. We are n the same fight.

One of the main objectives of being a successful dissident is to make the impersonal generic condemnation of others into a personal condemnation of you. Those who support the suppression of individual liberty and free market capitalism must understand that they are not allowed to criticize everything you believe in, and those who believe in it along with you, without simultaneously criticizing you. The supporters of suppression need to know that "others" and "you" are indivisible. This is a critical element of success.

It has been without much personal consequence that those who actively or passively support our oppression have been able to operate. We need them to face consequences. We need them to feel loss at a personal level. That loss is our relationship.

Learn to embrace the joy of losing. This seems counterintuitive, but the reasoning is simple. We're not going to win the battle for restored individual liberty in a single encounter or moment. There will be many battles and most, especially early on, will result in defeat. As established earlier, our enemy is formidable and well positioned. We need to realize that every time we engage in a dissident event, people are paying attention and our body of work is accumulating. When you lose, gather your group together, raise a toast, and say, "Well done. What a glorious defeat. Here's to our next effort!" Your losses are not in vain. Those losses will eventually lead to wins through perseverance.

Nowhere in the country has this been embraced better than in the tiny state of New Hampshire, where, beginning with an election challenge in Windham after November 2020, citizens have relentlessly been fighting for election integrity reform. At the time of this writing, they have been stymied at every turn for over three years. Each time, they have embraced the loss and then continued to fight on a brand-new front. Were they to be overcome with despair after their initial defeat, their movement would have long ceased its motion. Instead, it remains vibrant and active.

Play "small ball" and get involved at the local level. One of the curses of cable news is that we get to watch coverage of national and international events 24/7. We are treated to an endless stream of D.C. politicians and celebrity pundits talking about "big" issues.

An unfortunate by-product of this exposure to the big picture is that it makes the little picture seem mundane and boring. Local politics starts to feel beneath us. They aren't. They are what is all around us.

For anyone who might think elections were stolen, here is what I know: They could not have been stolen without the thieves controlling things on the ground at the local level. Run for city council. Volunteer to be a poll watcher. Get elected to the school board. It might not be glamorous and it might not land you on *Tucker Carlson*, but it is an effective way to work within the system and amplify your dissidence.

Take action in groups whenever possible. There is no great mystery to unravel here. We all know that, generally speaking, collective action is more powerful than just one individual acting alone. The problem we have as freedom-loving individuals is that sometimes taking group action feels counter to our nature. This is something we need to overcome. We are not in this alone and we can't get out of this alone.

In forming groups, think like firefighters—be ready when an alarm sounds. Everyone is familiar with the idea of groups forming to fight back against some certain issue or action. A group of business owners come together to fight an unreasonable zoning ordinance. A parents' group forms to fight an outrageous school board policy. From a dissident perspective, it can be effective to form a group and then watch for issues to present themselves. Have a trained and disciplined collection of dissident freedom fighters ready to take on any local act of oppression together. This will make you ready to mobilize and become "first responders" when the situation warrants.

Avoid defending yourself or justifying yourself to others—it's a trap. How often do you find yourself, when you're accused of being racist because of your political views, saying something like, "I'm not racist. I have three Black friends." How about when someone says you are a misogynist and you say, "I am not. I have three daughters and I treat them all with respect." We have let others put us on the defensive and make us feel as though we must answer their allegations on their terms. We do not.

When you are accused of being absolutely anything, do not defend yourself. Just look your accuser in the eye and say, "Your words, not mine."

Make predictions and let them be heard. We who believe in individual liberty and free market capitalism know what happens when both are strangled at the hands of the oppressive. We know what happens, but the average citizen does not. This means we can predict things that will happen and share those predictions with others. If generations of people can come to believe in horoscopes because of vague similarities between predictions and actual events, then they can certainly be made to believe in something when the predictions are specific and the events clearly take place.

Ask questions of those who are closest to you—don't argue with them! When you are with friends, family, classmates, coworkers, parish members, anyone who you find is in favor of suppression, ask them questions. Ask what they support, ask why they support it, ask them if they have considered X, Y, or Z. Force them to choose words to defend their beliefs. Don't try to force words upon them.

Every dissident gets out—no dissident is left behind. This is really tough. We all know of situations where someone around us has acted bravely and has then been persecuted as a result. We see this happen in the workplace, on university campuses, and in our own living rooms. When we watch someone being punished for standing up for liberty, we cannot just stand idly by and do nothing. Inaction is action. We have to put ourselves at risk and step in to support them. What is done to one is done to all. The time has passed for us to have the luxury of turning our backs and saying, "It's not my problem." It is your problem. It is our problem. We need to intervene. We have to do it rationally and constructively, but we have to do it. We also need to recognize that we will suffer some sort of consequence as a result of our action. Courage, one of the four classic virtues, must be summoned.

Don't recklessly martyr yourself. When Lech Wałęsa spoke of organizing his dissident activities in Poland, one of the points he made was that he did not want to produce martyrs unnecessarily. Poland had suffered enough and produced enough martyrs already in the twentieth century. Wałęsa said that he needed people who could work inside the system and make a difference without becoming objects of sacrifice.

We all know the person who says, "Watch what I'm going to post on Facebook. I guarantee they will take me down." Then they post. Then Facebook takes them down. Then they are out of the game. A martyr? Sure. Useful? Typically not.

Dissidents aren't pawns and they shouldn't be sacrificed. More specifically, they shouldn't needlessly sacrifice themselves. Choose your battles. Live to be a dissident another day.

Know that there will be martyrs as we move forward; call them such and keep track of them. Martyrs are those who fall to the abusive powers of the system. We are going to have the lives and careers of hundreds of thousands, if not millions, of people destroyed over the upcoming years. Let us make it a point not to lose track of them. We need to create lists—memorial "walls," if you will—that keep track of those who lose jobs, who lose scholarships, who lose their freedom, who might lose their lives. Eventually the lists of names will have weight. Weight is a destructive force, especially when being carried by a bloated and oppressive state.

Work within the limits of the system. It is more important to get something done than to have everything destroyed. Don't waste your time trying to be heard where you will be immediately silenced. Don't take on hopeless causes. Act as water would and follow paths of least resistance. We all know the destructive nature of a single dripping pipe in our home. Let the messages and actions flow where they can without containment.

Understand that your focus must be forward. Look where you are going, not where you have been. This is a warning directed to those who are obsessed with what was the clearly disturbing election process in November 2020 (and in some places like Arizona, again in 2022). It is also directed toward those who have become obsessed with various conspiracy notions over the past several years.

Without passing judgment on any of those claims or beliefs, I would suggest that if you want to prevail, dwelling on those things will not help the cause. You are not going to convince those in the circle below us to join us based on claims about that which might have happened. You will only convince them by having them understand what is happening now and what is likely to happen next. Leave the past and join the present. You are needed.

As an aside, the reason you can't convince them is because you don't actually have a "theory." You have a hypothesis. Taking election interference as an example, there are all sorts of data points that show various forms of tampering—both in 2020 and in 2022. The problem is that we can't yet prove that an election was stolen. We can use inductive logic, like Sherlock Holmes, to come up with a hypothesis, but not a theory. We cannot persuade others with a hypothesis because by its very definition a hypothesis has to be tested.

To go just a bit further with this, I have mentioned conspiracy theories a couple of times, and have just argued that they aren't theories at all but simply a collection of unproven hypotheses. There's a question as to why we seemingly have so many of them today. I believe there are three answers to that, and I want to share them here in this context because I believe they are worth everyone keeping in mind.

The first answer is that there aren't more of them; at least not as many more of them as we might think there are. The internet and social media have provided a means by which any sort of conspiratorial notion can grow like wild ivy. In the "old days," there was talk of conspiracy (and actual conspiracies formed) in every alehouse. Those were places where the actual seeds of our revolution were sown. Now they seem to proliferate but that might be a trick of our surroundings. Think of the pharmacist who comes home from work and says to his wife, "Honey, I'm worried. Everyone I saw today was sick. Something is going on."

The second reason is one offered by Charlie Kirk during the pandemic when he said that the things that are taking place in our country today seem so inexplicable to people that they simply have to construct something out of the ordinary to be able to explain it. They just cannot believe what they are seeing could possibly be happening without a grand plan of some sort behind it. I think there is a good deal of truth in that construct.

The final reason for the development of conspiracy ideas I believe can simply be found within our own nature—not in the stars but in ourselves.

When I speak before an audience, I like to try to show attendees that I'm "cultured" so I tell them I am going to show them some slides of very famous artwork. I get a humanities-literate volunteer to help me, and one at a time I show them four images, Each one is just collection of seemingly random dots on a blank background.

Nobody has ever been able to recognize these famous works of human ingenuity, creativity, and artistic talent.

Feeling both compassionate and a bit gleeful, I then say that I will give them some help and I put up a single slide with four different pictures displayed . . .

They are renderings of Taurus, Aries, Capricorn, and Gemini, set against a star-filled night sky, four signs known as signs of the Zodiac, and all created around a very loose formation of stars.

There is virtually no connection between these few stars in the sky and the complex constellation symbols that human beings were able to create. Perhaps the ancients were all on mushrooms, or maybe, just maybe, something more base-level was at work. I believe that humans are naturally inclined, perhaps obsessed, with making more of something than there actually is. We want to be the ones who "figure things out"—the ones who see what no one else can see. When there isn't really anything to see, we draw something. We connect dots. When there aren't enough dots, we add dots to connect.

Perhaps the answer lies both in the stars and in ourselves?

This makes us susceptible to manipulation by others. In 1705, the Anglo-Dutch social philosopher Bernard Mandeville anonymously published a satirical poem title "The Grumbling Hive: or, Knaves Turn'd Honest." It reappeared in different forms over time, but ultimately became called "The Fable of the Bees," one of the most important works of the early Enlightenment. I give it that distinction because of the incredible influence it would have on a variety of better-known thinkers, especially David Hume and Adam Smith. In the work, Mandeville brilliantly shows how bees destroy the hive when they abandon their own self-interest and instead focus on being "virtuous." Mandeville effectively argued how private vices support social benefits, an argument Smith especially would build upon in his *Wealth of Nations*.

I mention Mandeville's work as a hat tip and a recommendation for your own reading, but then as a segue to my own "fable of the bees" I use when speaking to audiences. It relates to conspiracies and the ease with which we can be manipulated. Imagine that you go on X (fka Twitter) tomorrow and you see a post by @BeeUScared. The anonymous name behind the handle points out that there is a report of someone dying from a bee sting near Kansas City and that the person had no known allergies. He urges people to keep an eye out. Seems strange.

The next day, a follower of @BeeUScared reports that they heard of a group of bees that got into a school bus filled with field trip students on their way to Cape Canaveral. Several students were hospitalized with severe reactions.

Over the next few days, the X group grows, and more and more people are reporting bee incidents, mostly ones about which they were told by someone else. Finally, someone reports another fatal bee sting reaction near Casa Grande, Arizona. @BeeUScared replies: "Likely US Feds experimenting with weaponizing bees? Anybody have info?"

Off we go.

There was once a constellation named for a bee called Musca Borealis. It no longer is recognized but that hasn't stopped us from potentially creating a whole new constellation. One that involves bees might seem trivial and harmless, but our desire to connect dots has been creating lots of trouble and will continue to do so until critical thinking and skepticism prevail.

Know when to push and know when to pull. Let's give a shape to this totalitarian beast we are facing and imagine it as an obelisk. A very large obelisk. Inside it, at its base, are the hard-core oppressors of individual liberty. As you go up inside the obelisk as it narrows, you find it filled with scattered passive supporters of our oppression. Together, the two groups live inside one large, seemingly impenetrable, stone tower.

There are two obvious ways to topple an obelisk. One is to get together enough force at the bottom and push it hard and fast until you cause it to tip over. The other is to throw a large rope around the top and pull it toward you until ultimately it falls.

But there is a third way to topple an obelisk. You can push and pull at the same time. As dissidents, we need to remember that many inside that obelisk are not actively seeking to control us. They are just complicit. We can find positive ways to engage them and reach them; to pull them toward us.

For those at the foundation of this massive structure, we know we need to push back. They act with intent to suppress our liberties. There will be no compromise or coming together with this lot. We need to push back against their efforts.

Do not expect instant gratification—steel yourselves for a long process. We got here over a century of decline. We will not reverse this in a couple of years. Pace yourself. Find ways to enjoy this gift that is life while still acting in your role as dissident. It does no good to abandon the joy of life while trying to improve life.

Call yourself a dissident and wear the label with honor. The other side, the oppressors, has long been winning the battle of language. It is time for us to take some control. Let us take the word "dissident" and ignore however and whoever else might have it in use and claim it for our own. We are the people who are dissenting from the prevailing direction of the country. We are the ones who are dissenting from limiting individual liberty and free market capitalism. Let us be united, clear, and unapologetic. Let us come under one term so we can speak with one voice and create a unified front for all other Americans to see.

Recruit members from our passive side into our active side. There are millions of people who will agree with us but who lack the willingness to join a dissident movement. As previously stated, we cannot force them, and we cannot reject them. We can, however, attempt to recruit them. Individually, in small groups, through our postings, we can try to get people to find the will inside themselves to join. This is our version of the "Great Commission." We need to go forth and bring others in. Having their support is helpful; having their active assistance may be the winning edge over time.

Make those newcomers feel welcome: Have you ever got talked into going to a party by a friend where you don't know anybody, but they assure you that they will stay with you and make you feel comfortable? What happens when you walk in the door? Your friend takes off immediately and leaves you standing alone wondering where to hang your jacket. It is a lonely, uncomfortable feeling and it makes you want to just turn around and leave.

As dissidents, we can't allow this to happen to new people who walk into our dissident "party." We need to make certain that they are welcomed warmly and introduced to the crowd. We don't want them to leave. If they do leave, they will return to the circle below us, or even worse, they may decide to join the oppressors in their circles. Every new dissident is a VIP upon arrival.

Remember that you are fighting for the restoration of the United States of America, not a restoration of the Trump presidency. While this might seem obvious, I don't believe that it will be to all people. It is easy to lose track. Many people in America have had a political awakening because of the pro-America candidacy and presidency of Donald Trump. For that, we should be grateful.

However, as we move forward, we must keep in mind that what we are trying to restore is something that is 230 years old, not something from 2016 to 2020. Place his picture on your wall if you'd like, but you will not be able to have people in the ring below us come to support us if they believe your ideas and your loyalties are attached to a man and not to a set of principles and values. This holds true even now in early 2024 as he runs for reelection. Make sure that if you are supporting his candidacy, you are doing so because you support his policies, not because you worship the man.

Share stories. We need to share the nature of our own persecution so that the stories are not just read or heard in the moment, but so that they accumulate. It will be the collective weight of those kinds of stories that can eventually help to break the back of a totalitarian state.

Learn to dine with new "friends"—remember they do not eat red meat. We are in the habit of mostly communicating about politics within the safety of our own ideological and philosophical circles. This is comfortable for us. We are going to need to get uncomfortable and start to engage people in the circle below ours who do not generally agree with us. That means that the kind of content we typically share, and the tone that we choose (especially on social media), not only will not work but will be counterproductive. "Red meat" can be served only to those who have a taste for it. Content that is both "leaner" and "sweeter" will be more appealing to the people we need to engage and persuade.

THIS HAS BEEN DONE BEFORE

We are not in uncharted territory. People have had their freedom taken and have been persecuted before. We are not used to seeing it happen in 4K resolution and in real-time using street-scene videos, but the general mechanics are all the same.

One thing that is quite different is that this totalitarian takeover is seemingly being led not by those in government, but by those in private industry, especially the media and big tech. It is not something that has ever really been anticipated by academics (only peripherally), and it seems counterintuitive that those who have profited from capitalism and liberty would want to attack both of those principles.

The Austrian School of Economic Theory has long held that the behavior of people in a free market is not explained by greed, as is often suggested, but by purposefulness. Even if your purpose is altruism, an Austrian would argue, you still must be able to produce something of value and sell it at a profit in order to give your profit away. What nobody has ever seriously contemplated is that the individual's "purpose" while participating in a free-market system might be to accumulate enough power to destroy the system.

Today's C-suite members certainly are not the great entrepreneurial champions of free markets who embrace traits of self-determination, creativity, and personal responsibility. They are not the Howard Roark or Hank Reardon prototypical and idealized warriors of capitalism created by Ayn Rand. Instead, these modern-day capitalists are like mercenary soldiers. They are paid to be in the fight but their loyalty lies only to dollars and not to ideas or values. They are not guarding a system of free exchange, they are milking it.

Whatever are the psychological explanations for this behavior, it might simply be reduced to their having a lust for power—a need to control. It seems that all roads ultimately lead back to Hobbes.

What we need to understand as Americans who value individual liberty and free market capitalism is that our role models are not George Washington, John Adams, and Thomas Paine. They can still be heroes, but for the situation in which we find ourselves, they cannot be role models. Their situation in 1776 does not truly resemble ours today. Their time is not our time.

Our role models need to be people like Lech Wałęsa, Aleksandr Solzhenitsyn, Natan Sharansky, and Andrei Sakharov. These were courageous men, true dissidents, who stood up to totalitarianism during the period of Soviet domination. Their unyielding yet steady courage and resolve helped to make the world understand what true oppression felt like. People forget that in the early days of Soviet Russia, the country was considered to be a utopian model for many in the West. The efforts of dissidents like these taught the world a different story. More importantly, over time it taught their countrymen.

It was their efforts, their sacrifice, and the sacrifices of others like them that eventually led to a bit of an incident in a shipyard in Gdansk.

We have an advantage over those in the past in counteracting this because we have more tools available to us in the early stages to start the dissident process. The bad news is that the oppressors also have more tools at their disposal. The conclusion is that the process will be long and trying. The door to our restoration is open but the ride will not be free.

Again, I have to stress the need for patience and acceptance; this is a long game. It is part of our psychology as humans to try to give meaning to our own lives by convincing ourselves that many things have started in our lifetime and those same things can end in our lifetime. We want this life we live to be somehow self-contained. In the case of American liberty, we have to understand that none of us were born when the deterioration started and few of us will likely be around to see its restoration. That means committing ourselves to a battle in which we likely won't live to see victory. That is hard. But as Ronald Reagan said, "If not us, who? If not now, when?"

Said in terms for fellow Game of Thrones followers: Winter is coming. Don a warm jacket, pick up a megaphone or a keyboard, start thinking up questions, and be prepared for a good deal of darkness to precede the light.

POSTSCRIPT

On March 11, 2022, it was my privilege to moderate a panel discussion composed of people who had been real-life dissidents fighting back against communism during the last century. The event, held at the Liberty Forum of Silicon Valley, had as participants Frank De Varona (Cuba), Sutton Van Vo (Vietnam), Peter Palecek (Czechoslovakia), Tatiana Menaker (Soviet Union), and Peter Wolf (East Germany).

The stories these courageous people told were unique to their experience but universal in their lessons. Despite the differences in countries and cultures, their experiences under totalitarianism were remarkably similar. Apparently, there are only so many ways in which to totally subjugate a people.

A highlight of the evening, which drew thunderous applause from the live audience, was when Tatiana Menaker gave her closing statement. In it, she said, in part:

The United States is not the country I immigrated to decades ago. It is now a nation of cowards. You need to remember that masters do not make slaves. Slaves make masters.
      Amen.

CHAPTER FOUR REFLECTIONS

What circle are you in?

_____

_____

_____

_____

_____

From the list in the chapter, is there anything you can choose from that you can do to get involved involved?

_____

_____

_____

_____

_____

Are there any ideas you have that are not mentioned?

_____

_____

_____

_____

_____

Set a plan for your own action and share it with at least one other person for accountability.

_____

_____

_____

_____

_____

CHAPTER FIVE:

AN IDEA ABOUT THE THIN LINE BETWEEN GOOD AND EVIL

"If only it were so simple! If only there were evil people somewhere insidiously committing evil deeds, and it were necessary only to separate them from the rest of us and destroy them. But the line dividing good and evil cuts through the heart of every human being. And who is willing to destroy a piece of his own heart?"
—Aleksandr Solzhenitsyn, *The Gulag Archipelago*

In the previous chapters in this book, I have attempted to take your box of preconceived ideas and dump it all over the floor for the purpose of getting you to reorder things. Much of what has been shared has been intended to have you look at issues and other people with a more open mind and a resharpened thought process. Now I'll ask you to put that to work by taking a fresh look not only at those who might heretofore be considered adversaries, but also at those whom you might consider to be allies. It will also force you to take a fresh look at yourself. Fair warning: You might not like what you see.

When I originally published this piece in January 2021 (and again revised and published on Human Events' website in 2023), I used it to make the argument that Team Left members have a slightly greater tendency to "cheat" in political matters, especially with regard to the election that had just taken place the previous November. Since then, I have had the opportunity to spend a good deal of time in and around various political grassroots organizations and events. My conclusion? While I found nothing to contradict my original contention, I have found an extraordinary amount of evidence that indicates that people who consider themselves to be "conservative" in their politics, referred to in this book as Team Right members, are absolutely no better than their liberal counterparts when it comes to behaving ethically.

In my associations with a wide range of Team Right organizations and individuals, I have witnessed personal betrayals in too many situations to count. I have seen money improperly taken from foundations meant to do good works. I have seen people lie about intentions strictly for the purpose of tricking and exploiting dedicated patriots. I have seen people who run "pro-America" organizations treat the people who work for them like garbage, finding reasons not to pay them for their services. Contracts get broken as if they were toothpicks.

Here is just some of what either I, or someone close to me, have witnessed in the movement from its leaders and their shills in just the past three years:

- An event being stolen away from the organizing group by an unscrupulous planner who kept the permits, and the event, for themselves.
- Money being taken from patriotic individuals in exchange for promises of speaking engagements and other opportunities that never materialized and the money never being repaid.
- Deliberate misrepresentation of news content by a major conservative media platform with a large and trusting following simply to get "clicks" and generate misplaced discontent.
- People willing to lie on behalf of organizations and change their recollections by 180 degrees simply to secure a paycheck.
- The outright hijacking and stealing of the efforts and ideas of honest patriotic citizens by someone simply to take the credit for themselves and profit.
- Individuals starting tax-exempt organizations as a means by which they can launder money, self-profit, or both.
- Public figures with loyal followings telling those citizens not to vote because the elections are rigged, which effectively surrenders that election to the other side.
- One movement "leader" asking another movement "leader" to lie under oath because their testimony would prove inconvenient for their own narrative.
- Religious leaders exploiting their flock by telling them that "what Jesus would do" would be to hate their enemy and worship themselves.

I have seen people turn in friends and "name names" relating to the preposterously labeled "insurrection" of January 6th simply to save their own skins or, even worse, just to harm others for their own personal glorification. Almost all of these actions to which I've borne witness have been undertaken by people who not only consider themselves to be conservatives in general, but who voted for Donald Trump in particular. This is not an indictment of Trump supporters. It is an indictment of humanity. Team Right members, conservatives, Trump supporters, are not inherently different at a personal level than any other person of any other political persuasion.

What all people are, regardless of their politics or positions, are humans, and humans generally don't behave well. It does beg the question that if one side's "we" are no better than the other side's "they" as the last three years have unequivocally proven to me, why then do some people seem to have a greater inclination and propensity to cheat?

I have a possible answer for that, and it isn't because of their politics or their "team."

As I have described, America is divided into two political teams: Team Right and Team Left. As we approach the 2024 election, many Team Right members are still trying to come to terms with the results of the 2020 election. They feel certain that Team Left cheated in a variety of ways in order to produce enough votes to secure victory.

Setting aside the MSM's agreed-upon talking points of "baseless accusations" of election fraud and their "despite there being no evidence to support such claims" mantra, we now know that there is significant evidence of election tampering. That is actually a "fact" where extensive work and research have been performed elsewhere. It is also, at this point, irrelevant. Joe Biden is in office. Focusing on 2020 election cheating is fine for investigators in various states if they so choose (there will be no federal investigation), but it is not helpful for ordinary citizens who would like to reverse trends.

The more helpful issue to explore in order to make a difference going forward is to answer the question posed above. We need to understand why some people seem to be more willing to cheat than others. It isn't about any group, or any person, being better or worse. It is about how their "worst" is inhibited. I believe that I can prove this by using a combination of reason and observation. Here we go.

I'M ETHICAL. ARE YOU ETHICAL?

Two terms that are tossed around quite frequently in arguments over political issues are "morals" and "ethics." For the purpose of this piece, I am going to consider them to be interchangeable, as anyone who tries to separate ethical considerations from helping determine what is moral and immoral conduct is in for a good deal of internal strife. There is some debate on this non-distinction within academic circles, but there are enough professionals in the field who would agree with me that I am not in a space that requires defending.

I have never in my entire adult life met a single person who says, "I am an unethical person." To the contrary, people universally assess themselves as being ethical. They also almost universally will agree that some number of "other people" are not ethical. If everyone says that they themselves are ethical, but at the same time says other people are not, then something must be wrong either with our understanding of ethics, or with our honesty about ourselves, or both. (Since the original publication of this piece, I have presented it to audiences many times. I always ask them, "How many people in this room think they are ethical?" They all raise their hands. I then ask: "How many people in this room think there are unethical people in the world?" Again, they all raise their hands. I then say, "Well, we are in a room filled with unicorns."

When the typical person says they are "ethical," they really mean that in their mind the things they do are the right things to do. This suggests a sort of self-legislating capability on the part of each person to know right from wrong. An idea like this can be found in the work of famous philosophers ranging from Immanuel Kant, to Karl Marx, and many others. They argue that each person is capable of such self-legislating and engage in the process constantly.

If this were the case, however, you would expect all people to reach the same conclusions as to what behaviors are acceptable and unacceptable. We empirically know this is not the case. We need look no further for proof than the above-referenced ethical assessment of individuals that goes: *I'm ethically okay, but they are not okay.*

If you ask a person the question "Are you ethical?" and they answer "yes," then the following question ought to be asked next:

Under what ethical system or construct do you define yourself as ethical?

Chances are, if you ask someone that question, the nine-out-of-ten-times response you will receive is, "Huh? What do you mean?"

Very few people realize that there are actual ethical systems that have been "constructed" to help direct us on the path to making consistent and appropriate decisions as to how to act and behave in any given situation. We have the above-referenced Kant's categorical imperative (if what I'm thinking of doing now were a rule that everyone had to follow, would it be workable for society?). We have Jeremy Bentham's utilitarianism (pure cost-benefit analysis) or John Stuart Mill's more refined and kinder version, which calls for cost-benefit analysis with an allowance for the subjective nature of "higher" human values.

We have, on the one hand, Objectivist ethics (my ethics) as given to us by the famous atheist Ayn Rand and as discussed in her essay "The Objectivist Ethics" (also expressed in John Galt's famous speech in the novel *Atlas Shrugged*). On the other hand, we have what is referred to as the Judeo-Christian ethic, although that does need some thin slicing as the teachings of Christ do materially refine the teachings that come from the Torah, Tanakh, or Old Testament. Islam and other religions also offer their own codes of ethical/moral conduct.

If none of those work for you, there is the self-sacrificing ethics of the French philosopher Auguste Comte and his coined term "altruism."

Finally, there are the observations of ethics and morality from a more empirical approach, like that of the Scottish Enlightenment's David Hume and Adam Smith, which in a simplified sense posit that we as humans develop ethical behaviors based upon the feedback we receive from others and their approval or disapproval.

There are a number of ways to view the development and deployment of moral and ethical behavior, but the typical person knows little, if any, of this. Yet they will tell you that they are ethical, and others are not. By what standard? How do they know? This logical dilemma, by the way, exists in people whether they were supporters of Donald Trump or Joe Biden; whether they are members of Team Right or Team Left. There is absolutely no difference in that respect. There is a difference we will get to eventually, but it is not universal and it does not involve ethics.

HOBBES WAS RIGHT!

It is my opinion, based upon many years of studying political philosophy, working in a large corporate environment, working with and running privately owned businesses, and doing political advising and writing, that the greatest of all the political philosophers, the one who got the most important thing right, was Englishman Thomas Hobbes. As mentioned earlier, legend has it that his mother went into premature labor out of fear of the approaching Spanish Armada. Hobbes spent the rest of his life focusing on the fearful nature of humans, among other things.

He is the father of social contract theory, which describes man's collective agreement to enter into civil society as a way to control his more primitive impulses. He is famous for his line about man's life in the state of nature, before the social contract, which he describes as being "solitary, poor, nasty, brutish, and short." Hobbes suggested that, owing to their nature, men are unable to be left to govern themselves without stern direction. His diagnosis of us as people? Fearful and self-destructive. His prescription? A strong sovereign.

Hobbes is also the father of the idea of moral relativism. His contention is that, for the typical human, their calculation of whether or not something is "right or wrong" is nothing more than a reduction to looking at things that please them and things that offend them. They maximize the one and avoid the other. In that process, they create their own morality, or set of ethics, that is based solely upon their own desires and aversions.

My own life of study and empirical observations have led me to conclude that this theory of human behavior and ethical development most accurately describes the greatest number of people. Assuming a human population existing under a bell curve, Hobbes's ethical construct describes the greatest number of people gathered around the mean.

I want to take a brief writer's "rest area" exit and pause to comment on my Hobbes defense above in conjunction with the ideas of ethics/morals given to us by Adam Smith that were also briefly referenced. I have the utmost regard for Adam Smith and his insights, in particular those found in *The Theory of Moral Sentiments*, his less widely known precedent to the *Wealth of Nations*, Smith contends that ethical behavior is to some extent embedded naturally in the human conscientiousness and that our natural instinct is reinforced and perfected through our interactions with others. The more interactions we have, the better we will get. That actually makes some sense.

Now, however, we are back to our nature and my view of Hobbes's position. It does seem clear to me that we are learning things and that it is through our interactions with others we come to understand what kinds of behavior will tend to please them and not give offense. Said another way, we learn how to behave in a way that won't encourage others to harm us. I believe that Smith is right about how we learn, but Hobbes explains how we use that knowledge. We do not necessarily use it with the positive intention of doing good, or at least no harm, to others. We use it for the purpose of knowing how to manipulate others. Our ethics essentially become a corset on a World War I German general—something to disguise our grotesque bulges and improve our outward appearance. They are used to disguise our reality.

One more point on Smith, who was quite presciently writing in the late-middle part of the eighteenth century. Smith was concerned about the impact of living in large cities on our ethics/morality. He felt that large cities took away from the personalization of our connections with others and made it easier for what I will term "bad behavior" to go without detection or consequence. Now consider today's America. We have many large cities with populations of hundreds of thousands, even into millions. We have very large corporations, some with populations in the tens of thousands. Finally, we have the various worldwide social media "communities." Americans today can occupy not one, not two, but potentially three large communities. What might Smith have said about the impact that would have upon our ethical behavior?

This points us in the direction of contemplating the importance of consequences. The larger the group, the less likely is the perpetrator of bad behavior to be "punished" for their actions. We hold ourselves and our immediate loved one to a higher standard because we are right here! There is no place to hide. The larger the environment, the easier it becomes to behave badly and perhaps go unnoticed and thereby unpunished. No consequences.

We do fear consequences and adapt accordingly. It was none other than the father of psychoanalysis, Sigmund Freud, who in his superb sociological work *Civilization and Its Discontents* argued that civil society forces man to suppress, to sublimate, his true base-level desires (very Hobbesian) in order to coexist with others. If I put Freud together with Smith together with Hobbes, I think it is fair to ask how good a job is today's American doing at sublimating?

This is a good place to pause and share the warning I have been expressing for the past half-decade regarding artificial intelligence (AI) and ethics. I think this is perhaps the most serious of the undiscussed issues facing us today. I say it faces us today because the problem is down the road, but only addressing it today can prevent it tomorrow. Tomorrow will be too late.

Much time is spent focusing on the "intelligence" part of AI: what it can do, the tasks it can simplify, the leisure time it will create. Nowhere near enough time is spent focusing on the "artificial" component. What can we expect in terms of artificial ethics?

The proponents of AI tout a system's capacity to learn. Yuval Noah Harari and those like him seem to think AI systems might even replace us at some point. If they do, problem solved, I guess, a sort of "final solution" for all of humanity. My concern is what happens during an interim period of unknown duration. Specifically, if these things are capable of learning, what might they learn about ethics?

The machine-turns-on-man scenario is well known to fans of science or apocalyptic fiction. Starting perhaps with HAL in *2001: A Space Odyssey* refusing to open the pod bay doors, to Arnold Schwarzenegger and "I'll be back" in the *Terminator* film series with the rise of the machines, creative minds have imagined a world where computers take control of the human experience. Now a fresh set of minds has begun to turn fiction into reality. As they do, these AI contraptions are being programmed to "think."

How does that programming work? Are they being programmed with a specific set of ethics? Are they Objectivists (I personally hope so because then we have nothing to fear)? Are they utilitarian? If they are, how do they calculate costs and benefits? Are they using the categorical imperative to self-legislate (if this were a rule for all, would it be workable for society)? The problem there, as has been pointed out over nearly 200 years, is that everything hinges on how you ask the question. You can set it up to really get any answer you want. Will AI systems perhaps be fully altruistic and find themselves constantly rebooting and sacrificing themselves for the sake of others?

My guess is that they are going to "learn" how to behave ethically, just like most humans do. That means we have to address the inherent nature of an AI system: fundamentally good or evil? I am completely incapable of making such an assessment, and I wonder if the people designing these systems can truly answer the question either. Will AI systems be like the inherently good and ever-learning-with-experience person about whom Adam Smith wrote, or will AI systems be some techno-combination of Hobbes's and Freud's man, pure moral relativists weighing merely their own pleasure and pain? As I mentioned at the very outset of this book, free markets tend to do best when they are in the process of discovering. Once humans have developed something, however, all bets are off.

Will these artificial systems being designed to be "better" and more efficient than us be able to rise above us in terms of consistent ethical behavior and elevate us in the process, or will they simply rise above us in their ability to manipulate, rationalize, exploit, and outright harm both us and their fellow machines? Stay tuned and stay alert.

Back to our story. At this point you might think I'm suggesting that Biden supporters and Team Left members are more likely to be moral relativists than are Trump supporters and Team Right members. That somehow I believe Team Right members are inherently better creatures.. You'd be wrong. I am not. I believe that most people are moral relativists in general, and even that people who attempt to operate under a more disciplined structure of ethics, including the Christian ethic, can become moral relativists at the very moment that they find themselves placed most at risk.

Survival is in our nature. When it is in jeopardy, even the most professed or truly righteous may attempt to hedge their ethical bets.

Ethics are interesting things. For the most part, we don't really need them in our daily lives. Most of the routine decisions and encounters we face do not present ethical dilemmas. The reason we need ethics is that when we find ourselves in difficult positions, absent a system to which we can turn, we are left entirely on our own. In that moment, most people will simply make a decision that maximizes their own pleasure and minimizes their own pain regardless of the consequences or the impact on others.

For the typical person, and as discussed above in the digression involving Smith and Hobbes, they have a general understanding of behaviors that will either ingratiate them to others or have them be rejected. They will try, to varying degrees, to engage in the kinds of behaviors that "do no harm." However, most people have a limit as to how far they can, or will, go in their attempt to stay in the good graces of those around them. Everyone's limit is different. Have you ever said to somebody, "I can't believe that John/Jane did that. I never expected that from them. It seems completely out of character"? When you say that, what you are experiencing is John/Jane reaching their limit of how far they could go before turning into a simple moral relativist.

I had the occasion within the past decade to work very closely with someone who became not only a trusted and capable business colleague, but also a valued friend. He was introduced into my world by a personal friend of his who was also a business partner of my client. When the business partnership went off the rails, my colleague looked at the facts, came to the conclusion that it was his own friend who had not honored their commitments, and while suffering damage to that personal friendship, he did the right thing professionally with regard to how he handled the winding down of the relationship between his friend and my client. Well done.

Then, more than a year later, he and I again found ourselves involved in similar circumstances with people around us behaving very badly. Only this time, there was a significant amount of money involved. I will only say that the choices my friend made in that moment were exactly 180 degrees away from the ones I watched him make only less than two years earlier. It seemed out of character. I never expected it from him. He had reached his limit.

I believe it is impossible to argue that there is any fundamental difference in ethics between the typical Trump or the typical Biden supporter. If there is no fundamental difference, why go through all the trouble to share this background on ethics? It is for the purpose of helping to understand why some are more likely to cheat in matters of political activity than others, and why I feel there might be a slightly greater propensity on the part of Team Left members to do so.

To support my claim and understand why this is, I believe we need to look beyond ethics and consider Tom Hanks, World War II, and the ancient Stoics.

DUTY AS A DIFFERENTIATOR

Love or hate his personal life and politics, Tom Hanks makes spectacular movies and is especially good in war roles. A few years back, I had a chance to watch him in the Apple Television release of *Greyhound*. It is a story based on the U.S. Navy convoys that brought supplies and armaments across the Atlantic during World War II. It is not a long film, but it is nonstop action-packed. For ninety minutes, there is nothing but German U-boat peril. American sailors show incredible courage, some losing their lives, others saving lives, while up against challenging odds.

In the end, the convoy clears the danger with some loss of cargo and life but primarily intact. The gallantry and sacrifice of the men on the ships translated into a victory for the Allies at that moment.

As I watched the film, I couldn't help but think that when the War was over and those young men returned home to their lives and loved ones, some of them would go on to live lives of great honor. Others, however, would certainly go on to become compulsive gamblers, beat their wives, beat their children, steal from their business partner, rob the local gas station, etc. I recently had occasion to work with a business where one partner, an ex–U.S. Marine, stole over $500,000 from the other partner.

What happens to make men so courageous in one moment and so devoid of any kind of ethical or moral compass in the next? I think the answer lies in the notion of duty. Those men on the ship with Tom Hanks in that movie were driven in those moments by a higher calling. They had a sense of duty. Some, when they returned home, for whatever reason, might have lost their way; they found themselves left with no higher calling. Absent duty, they were left with only their own personal moral and ethical framework in which to operate. Given moral relativism, they became able to justify almost any behavior.

This notion of duty is a very Stoic concept. Stoicism, which dates back to Ancient Greece, emphasizes duty and the importance of virtue. There were four attributes of virtue: wisdom, justice, courage, and moderation. Doing one's duty was central to the Stoics. Duty manifested itself in more than just following orders; it meant adhering to the four key elements of virtue and to keeping in sync with all of nature.

One does not have to buy into all of Stoic philosophy to grasp the importance of duty. It is with duty that we can begin to answer the question of why do some people seem more inclined to cheat in political matters than others, and why do Team left members seem to be slightly even more inclined to cheat than do Team Right members?

It is because people will cheat more readily when they lack a sense of duty to something *outside* themselves *and* that has an *objective* foundation. The contemporary Team Left member is a bit less likely to have any external force that commands them to "behave better."

Again, operating under the bell curve, the mainstream Team Right member is a bit more likely to profess to follow either the voice of God, the call of patriotism, or both. Both are external to themselves. Both set standards for behavior that transcend their own personal calculations of convenience. Both provide fairly clear direction, either through Scripture or the Constitution. Both rest like weights upon their shoulders, burdening them with a non-ignorable sense of obligation.

It is without any reservation that I qualify a reverence for the Constitution as being objectively linked to patriotism. Consider for a moment what it means to say that someone either loves or hates their country. Does it mean they love/hate real estate? Does it mean they love/hate the 330 million or so inhabitants? Does it mean that they love/hate rap music or Chicago-style pizza? The only objective thing we can take it to mean as a way to deal with it is that they either love or hate the Constitution as originally drafted and subsequently amended. (It is always important to remember, and conveniently forgotten, that amendments to the Constitution are just as much a part of it as if they were included from the beginning. In other words, slavery is unconstitutional. It is simply an intellectually vapid reference to say that our Founders originally provided for its use so our Constitution is flawed from the outset.)

My calculation is simple but not simplistic. If an American feels a sense of patriotic duty, then by definition the Constitution becomes that external objective document, independent of himself, which informs his conscience.

It is the Constitution, nothing more and nothing less, that does make America "exceptional" to whatever extent that might still be true. If there ever was any special sort of "explorer gene" that accounted for the adventurous and expansionist settlement of our nation, it has long since recessed. Americans are simply members of the human race, members who have shown a propensity to do all of the same awful things to one another as do humans elsewhere. What separates us is the foundation of our system, not our behavior within it. No matter the system of government, you will always have lawbreakers and bad actors, *ergo*, the system is what is most important. Our Constitution gave us the best ever, both as conveyed and implemented.

Like the Constitution, sacred Scripture serves the same purpose for someone who claims a sense of duty to God. (Notice I wrote "claims." I will come back to that.) As someone in recovery, I am fully aware of the concept of having one's "higher power" being a doorknob. Any purported reverence to God that excludes a requirement to reference an actual Scripture allows the moral relativist present in all of us to turn God into a hooker in Times Square at 2:00 a.m. back in 1978: God can be anything you want Him to be.

For those who have this sense of duty to either God or country, it doesn't mean they won't fail. It doesn't mean they will not behave badly. It simply means they have a better chance of making a better choice than a person who is not encumbered by any sense of duty other than to themselves. Duty is typically viewed as a call to act. It can just as easily be seen as the antithesis to action, which means it can inhibit. "I must because it's my duty. I must not because it betrays my duty."

Here I want to emphasize and expound upon what I mentioned at the outset. I do not believe for a second that Team Right members are more ethical than Team Left members. They are both equally unethical. What you will find is that just, *en masse*, there are more Team Left members who will deemphasize the importance of either Scripture or the Constitution than there are Team Right members. Verifying that assertion is the easiest Google you can find. Recent polling from General Social Survey on religious affiliation and Rasmussen on Constitutional perceptions give clear support to the contention. That doesn't mean Team Right members are better Judeo-Christians or better Americans. It just means they are a bit more likely to feel guilty about committing acts of unrestrained aggression (you don't have to be violent to be aggressive).

The exceptions to this rule are everywhere. That is why I'm trying to be clear that no political side is inherently better than the other. I see religion and patriotism as simply being inhibitors of unethical behavior. I have found many people who profess to be Christians to behave quite badly, as do many people who profess to be patriotic. I have almost come to fear people who call themselves "God-fearing Americans." That said, strong belief in either God or country do seem to impose a degree of restraint upon actions. The sin of thought gets translated into the sin of action just a bit less often.

But just a bit.

When I ask someone who does not tie himself too tightly, or at all, to either duty to country or Scripture to what might they hold a sense of duty, their responses generally fall into one of three categories:

- I have a duty to those around me.
- I have a duty to those less fortunate than myself.
- I have a duty to humanity.

The shared characteristic of each of those "duties" is that although they sound as if they reside "outside" the individual, they are wholly subjective with regard to their definition. Each individual person gets to define their "duty to others" however they see fit. There is no separate standard. As I have established, for those focused on a Christian duty, there is the reasonable clarity of the Bible. For those who pledge allegiance to the United States of America, there is our Constitution bolstered by the original Declaration of Independence.

For those, however, who say that they simply have a duty to help "others," the others can be whomever they so choose, and need whatever kind of help it is the helper decides they should provide.

Machiavelli provides the final element.

To succinctly summarize my thoughts to this point, it is my personal belief that the members of Team Right are not inherently any more ethical than are their counterparts on Team Left. When it comes right down to it, individual to individual, most people are basic moral relativists as identified and defined by Hobbes, and given no other considerations, most people conduct themselves under an ethical code that is simply one of convenience.

The difference between the two is that those who answer to a calling of duty that is outside themselves and more objective than subjective in nature can have their individual passions held in check. It gives their better angels a chance to be heard and followed.

Now to directly address the question asked at the beginning of this chapter, which was why do some people seem to have a greater propensity to cheat than do others? The answer is found in the writings of the fifteenth-century philosopher Machiavelli and his short, world-changing book entitled *The Prince*.

Machiavelli is the one who gave us the phrase "The ends justify the means." The pragmatic (general use of the term), realistic, almost sociopathic philosopher set the standard for tough love that needed to be applied by a Prince. Certainly, Hobbes was greatly influenced by his work.

Machiavelli's statement about ends and means explains why the modern-day Team Left member, almost always a Democrat, *might* be *a bit more willing* to cheat. Existing as a typical moral relativist where little to nothing is *malum in se*, and being for the most part unconstrained by a sense of duty other than that which they conveniently self-define, any sort of activity is permissible so long as they end up getting what they want. They give cover to this behavior by saying their actions are necessary to "help others." As has been shown, that statement can mean whatever they want it to mean. Team Right members do this, too, and I have been both a personal and a professional victim of their own Machiavellian maneuvers.

By our nature as humans, we are flawed and sinful creatures. That goes for Trump supporters as well as those who lined up behind Joe Biden. The difference is that for those of us who truly have a good old-fashioned love for God, country, or both, we have a voice outside ourselves warning us to control our nature. It asks us to heed a higher calling. It limits us in a way that is beneficial to maintaining an ordered, predictable, and just society. This does not mean that people professing to have a strong belief in Scripture or the Constitution are especially superior "God followers" or Americans. It simply means they might feel that they ought to be. The "ought" in this case can potentially impact the "is" in a positive manner.

Very succinctly, the difference between a cheater and a non-cheater in the political social realm most often comes down to a simple hounding from external conscience not from internally developed ethics.

Those who operate without that sense of duty, that conscience, are left to do whatever their free will wishes, unbound by any real constraints. They can justify their actions through the simple pleasure they feel or the pain they avoid. Their ends always can justify their means.

That is why they cheat. That is how we can use our reason to know they cheat.

WHAT CAN BE DONE (. . . IF ANYTHING)?

The great problem in attempting to navigate an unethical political-social terrain is that it is very difficult to know whom to trust and how to organize your own activities without allowing all that matters to you to become corrupted. With that in mind, I offer some suggestions below as to things to keep in mind when engaging in civic activities. Before I get there, allow me to make my strongest suggestion.

If you do not have one already, search for and find an ethical system that you can understand, adopt, and rely upon in difficult moments. For me, Objectivist ethics have been the crutch upon which I lean in challenging situations. In finding your way, I will suggest that the best test to determine if an ethical system works is that, if put to use in a difficult moment, it doesn't simply yield a result that either maximizes your pleasure or minimizes your pain. A proper system will have you adhere to a process that leads to a result. It won't let you pick a result and then let you rationalize a process.

Once you have your system and your ethical feet are firmly planted, here are some things to keep in mind when encountering others in your political-social endeavors. I implore you to be less trusting. It isn't a comfortable way to live, but if you really care about changing the course of the country, then you need to force yourself to gaze upon those around you, those professing to lead you, with a jaundiced eye. The following tips come from my own real-life experience and the real hard lessons learned as a result:

- Don't let dollar signs cloud your vision. Do not surrender your group's mission or vision or let it be compromised over the promise of funding from some large benefactor or organization.
- Be careful about buying products where you are led to believe that some portion of the proceeds are going to a cause in which you believe. I can assure you it isn't necessarily true.
- Those who talk in platitudes generally lack gratitude and carry a bad attitude. If you like clever rhyming, use it as a way to remember to avoid those who talk the loudest and who present the boldest. They are often just leeches in wolf's clothing.
- Avoid people who use their own martyrdom in order to promote themselves. Remember, martyrs typically don't live to tell their story. Be wary of those who have.
- Beware of people encouraging you to take risks on their behalf while they sit upon a safe perch. Don't let them pick you up by your ankles and use you to beat their nemesis over the head.
- Don't put anybody on a pedestal. You might like what someone appears to be doing or what you hear them saying but don't transgress into idol worship. Too many of these leaders in political movements have built a cult-like following. That was bad in Guyana and it's bad here, too.
- Listen very carefully when someone starts to tell you what your "duty is as a Christian." Oftentimes those who wear Christ on their sleeve carry something else, something darker and manipulative, in their hearts. If you are truly a Christian, you don't need somebody to tell you what Jesus wants you to do. You already know.
- The exact same warning given above pertains to those who tell what is your "patriotic duty." Be especially careful if their instructions to you are followed by a "Click here to donate" button.

Do not let yourself be compromised in your own ethics by associating with someone whose behavior is clearly unethical under any system, but who happens to agree with you on issues. The phrase "The enemy of my enemy is my friend" should be banished from your lexicon. It works with geopolitical war (siding with Stalin against Hitler), but in everyday civil society it leads to incivility, and it leads to you compromising who and what you are out of simple convenience.

There is a great expression that goes, "Keep your friends close and your enemies closer." Great expression. Bad idea, at least in this case. I hope everyone reading this takes a step back, if for just a moment, and checks their premises about everything they are doing and everyone they are following. If you see the signs of corruption in someone in the public square, especially in leadership roles, trust your instincts. Step back and step away. Resist the siren's song filled with inspiring chords and lofty lyrics. It is just a song. Nothing more. Backstage those performers are laughing at you. They are calling you suckers and planning on how they can fool you with their next trick.

That last sentence is one you need to sit with for more than a moment. If you succeed in shoring yourself up ethically, you need to understand that others may come to see your resolve and absolute standards as a weakness, and they will attempt to find ways to exploit it and take advantage of it. They will see your unwillingness to break your vows to yourself as a way to manipulate and exploit you. Remember this: If they attempt to take advantage of your ethical inflexibility, whatever it is they might be able to take, they cannot take you. Not if you hold fast to yourself. Remember, the only person in the world who really knows who and what you are is you. If you lose sight, nobody is left to know.

Here is the saddest part of what has happened to us as a people. We have become so obsessed in this country with the need to make all things political, and we have become so eager to compete with and confront others, that we are deciding what defines a person by for what and for whom they vote. We have literally assigned labels of good and evil to people based upon the yard signs they display during even numbered years (odd years for many municipalities). This leads us to make enormous errors in judgment about people in both directions. I have come to the conclusion over time that not only does how someone votes tell you little about what kind of person they are, it actually tells you *nothing* about what kind of person they are. We need to look more deeply into people. We need to look deeper into ourselves.

The question we all have to ask is: When I look at myself do I see the man (or woman) I wanted to be, or somewhere along the line did I slip off track? Virtually no one wants to be unethical and virtually nobody thinks they are. Our behavior informs us otherwise. Do better.

CHAPTER FIVE REFLECTIONS

Do you think you're ethical? If so, why?

_____

_____

_____

_____

_____

Are there any of the different systems mentioned in the chapter you'd like to learn more about? Pick one and make some notes.

_____

_____

_____

_____

_____

Think of situations you were in where you made a choice you later regretted-not because it didn't work, but because you didn't feel good about it. What should you have done differently and why?

_____

_____

_____

_____

A DECLINATION OF CODEPENDENCE

(or . . . Are you willing to take off your shoes?)

*"And dying in your beds, many years from now, would you
be willing to trade all the days, from this day to that, for one
chance, just one chance, to come back here, and tell our enemies,
'You may take our lives, but you'll never take our freedom'!"*
—Mel Gibson portraying William Wallace in the motion picture
Braveheart

In mid-July of 2021, I had the opportunity to be the featured speaker for the Liberty Forum of Silicon Valley at the invitation of Jane Kearney. The group has acquired a reputation over time as a place where any individual should consider themselves honored to be asked to step to the podium. While to this day I'm convinced that when they invited me, they must have thought I was somebody else, I was certainly humbled nonetheless.

The title of the talk was "The Dissident's Fight for Freedom in 21st-Century America," and it was a synthesis of a couple of essays I had published back in January of that year on my own website: one on the topic of political ethics (revised and included in this collection) and the other specifically about being an American dissident (revised and included in this collection). It was well received, drawing two humbling standing ovations at the conclusion.

The presentation ended with my sharing a story from a patriotic dissident event that had taken place over the recent Fourth of July weekend in South Dakota. That event, which was covered in the run-up to it by my Human Events platform, faced aggressive suppression and censorship on social media, and was a microcosm of the challenges we face as we struggle against the ever-strengthening forces of collectivism.

The actual and slightly allegorical story I shared was that of the event organizer, my dear friend Felisa Blazek, having to literally run barefoot over gravel, and at full speed, while chasing down an automobile filled with a family who had just been turned away at the event gate by being told "they were not on the list." The family was, in fact, "on the list" and were being denied entrance in what can only be considered a deliberate act of sabotage. It is exactly the sort of thing that we dissidents need to expect and be prepared to deal with as we continue our fight to alter the current trajectory of America.

Felisa caught the family, got them admitted into the event, and tore up both feet in the process. At that moment, she thought there was nothing significant about what she had done. Later that day when she shared what had happened, someone asked her why she did what she did, running across gravel barefoot to chase down a car while showing no regard for her own personal well-being. She simply responded, "What else was I supposed to do? They are patriots. I had to do something."

The metaphor from the story was clear. Given the current state of our country, for those who wish to join in the struggle to restore individual liberty, we are going to have to be willing to take off our shoes and run on the rocks. We are going to have to take risks. We are going to have to expose ourselves to the potential to suffer both pain and loss on a very personal level.

At the conclusion of my Liberty Forum presentation, having shared the "run barefoot on the rocks" story, an audience member with an Eastern European accent by the name of Peter Palecek approached me to shake my hand. He shared that he had been a dissident student in Prague in 1968 when the Soviet tanks rolled in to crush an uprising known famously as the Prague Spring. He commended my talk but said that the story at the end particularly had moved him. He said that story had brought it all back to him again. I guess it reminded him of all the rocks he and his fellow dissidents had metaphorically run across barefoot.

Peter's response gave the inspiration for a panel event being held the following March at the Liberty Forum of Silicon Valley. Co-hosted by Human Events and planned by the run-on-the-rocks lady herself, we assembled six real-life dissidents from East Germany, Soviet Union, Czechoslovakia (Peter Palecek), Cuba, and Vietnam. By all recollections, it was the first event of its kind ever held. A special evening and a chance to marvel at the impact that can come from a simple story being told.

For this dissident, who was fortunate enough to be a featured speaker on the main stage in South Dakota July 3, 2021, the event was an almost Homeric experience. Along the way we encountered heroes, villains, unexpected adversity, uplifting moments, grotesque oddities, and pleasant wonders. There were people who abandoned commitments, people who rose above and beyond, people who sabotaged, and people who did exactly what they were supposed to do. By Sunday, in its final manifestation, it had become an almost spiritual gathering of like-minded, patriotic souls, wearing freedom's dirty shirt, who were able to feel safe and share in a common experience free of the judgment, ridicule, and shame they might encounter in the outside world from family, friends, and coworkers.

The South Dakota event became like a 12-Step meeting for recovering Americans. Or perhaps, for Americans trying to recover. There is more than just safety in numbers; there is also strength and inspiration to be found. As we look to the recent history of Eastern Europe and the various dissident movements that ultimately prevailed through perseverance, the unity found in group activity is a critical element for success. Dissidents need one another not just for efficacy, but for their very sanity.

Again, the implication of the story I told is clear. If you believe in liberty and if you are inclined to join in with the active dissident movement in this country, please, take off your shoes. Run barefoot on the rocks. We will not gain as a dissident movement without experiencing some degree of pain.

What follows is the speech I gave on that Saturday night in South Dakota, a speech designed to encourage people to show individual courage and stand up for themselves.

A speech designed to have them take off their shoes.

AMERICAN DECLINATION OF CODEPENDENCE

Issued July 4th, 2021

PREAMBLE

It was 245 years ago that a brave group of American colonists sent what was effectively a legal complaint to the King of England. Inspired in part by the English jurist William Blackstone, the complaint contained a list of the colonists' grievances and then demanded their independence as a sort of compensation for damages. This citizen's complaint is commonly known as the Declaration of Independence.

We celebrate July 4, 1776, as our nation's birthday. It is not, in the strictest sense, the date of our birth, nor is it even the actual year. Depending on how you choose to define it, our nation was actually "born" either in 1787 (signing of the Constitution), 1788 (ratification of the Constitution), or 1789 (convening of the First Congress). What then should we call July 4, 1776? It is the day we got pregnant. What followed was a long and bloody path toward liberation and birth.

Today, the Declaration of Independence is one of the—if not the—most cherished American documents. Its language is inspiring, and it reminds us of the incredible courage shown, and the price paid, by those who risked and gave all in order to secure for us the gift of freedom. It is a foundational part of our history.

But it is not a part of our present. We no longer are a distant colony living under the rule of an unreasonable king. We won our freedom, wrote a Constitution, and built a new nation. Using the greatest ideas from the Enlightenment, our Founding Fathers started us on a path that led us to become the greatest nation in the history of Western Civilization.

We won our independence, but we now suffer under a new sort of tyrant. We find ourselves bound by the invisible chains of codependence. We are not being ruled unreasonably by others. Instead, we are unreasonably letting ourselves be ruled by the need to appear caring and helpful in supporting, perpetuating, and enabling the irresponsible and destructive behavior of our fellow citizens who are determined to fundamentally transform the tenets of Americanism.

It is, therefore, once again time for a statement to be made and for lines to be drawn. We cannot find the strength to restore our republic if we cannot first find the strength to set our own minds, bodies, and consciences free. It is time to formally, and publicly, decline to remain codependent.

THE DECLINATION

When in the course of human events, it becomes necessary for a group of people, who believe in the laws of nature and in nature's God, to dissolve the codependent bands that, to their own great detriment, have connected them to others, a decent respect to the opinions of mankind requires that they should list the actions they intend to take in separation and rebellion.

Let it first be clear: We hold these truths to be self-evident:

- That all Americans are created equal.
- That they are endowed by their Creator with, and have had codified in their Constitution, certain inalienable rights. These include: the right to life, liberty, the pursuit of happiness, and the right to act as we choose insofar as we do not compel others to act as we choose.
- That these rights have been gradually eroded, both through public seizure and voluntary surrender.
- . . . And that to continue to allow those rights to be denied to us by others, or worse, to voluntarily surrender our rights for the sake of, and in appeasement to others, is immoral.

Since our present circumstance has become destructive toward the abovementioned truths, it is the right of the American people to abolish the current state of affairs and to institute a new order based upon:

- Self-understanding
- Self-respect
- Self-confidence
- Self-determination
- Self-preservation

History has shown that people are more disposed to suffer and stay silent while evils are sufferable than they are to stand up and fight back. With respect to their perception vis-à-vis others, they also are inclined to be governed and inhibited by three types of fear:

- The fear of losing something they think they have
- The fear of not getting something they want
- The fear of not being liked

These fears can lead a free people to subjugate their own free will to a sort of social codependence that erodes their freedoms and weakens their very God-given souls.

But when a long train of abuses, usurpations, oppression, and persistent censorship leaves them no alternative action to be taken, then it is their right, their duty, to throw off such suppression and their inhibitions.

Today's committed Americans have spent so much time trying to prove who and what they are not, that they have forgotten who and what they are. That ends now.

Therefore, we are resolved that from this moment forward, in declining our codependence upon those who do not hold to our truths, that . . .

𝔚𝔢 𝔖𝔥𝔞𝔩𝔩...

1. Break loose from the self-fitted chains and shackles of political correctness.
2. Take back our language. No longer will we surrender words and phrases from our language to others. We will use the words we choose to use regardless of their contemporary characterization or classification by others.
3. Not be made to condemn or apologize for the actions of others. Likewise, we will not be made to applaud or affirm the behavior of others. We will apologize only for our own actions when we feel it appropriate, and we will salute others only when we are personally so moved.
4. Never deny our friendships or turn our backs on those of us who are being attacked by others simply because it is easier, convenient, or avoids confrontation.
5. In accordance with the above, we will not hesitate to intervene in a situationally appropriate manner when we see one of our fellow citizens coming under attack. To turn away is to become complicit.
6. Let those around us know that when they attack any one of us, they attack all of us. We will not tolerate the phrase "But I didn't mean you."
7. Embrace the classical notions of being masculine and feminine whenever and however we choose, and we shall not make excuses or issue apologies for so doing.
8. Be skeptics at every turn when someone claims to be an "expert," an "authority," or a "follower of science."

9. Not allow ourselves ever to use the excuse of "I was just following orders" to serve as a reason for engaging in helping to silence or harm our fellow citizens.

10. Not engage in defending ourselves when we are called racist, when we are called homophobic, when we are called privileged, when we are called xenophobic, or when we are labeled by anyone other than ourselves. We will not respond by giving examples of people we know or things we have done to prove what we are and what we are not. We do not need to try to justify ourselves or disprove baseless accusations to others. We will simply respond, "Your words. Not mine."

11. Embrace our faith in God, if we possess such faith, without reservation. We may wear it on our sleeves, or we may keep it to ourselves. We will display our faith however we so choose and will not deny the existence or importance of our faith for the sake of providing false comfort to others.

12. 12. Refuse to acknowledge the need for, and legitimacy of, "safe spaces" or "microaggressions." Simply because someone else decides they are threatened or offended will not be a reason for us to question our beliefs, our words, or our actions.

13. Call "lies" by their proper name, which is "lies."

14. Not give the benefit of the doubt to those who seek to silence us or control us by presuming they are of good intentions. We will take them at their word and assume they mean and intend exactly what they say.

15. Take great care in using terms such as "courage" and "bravery," understanding that those terms have become corrupted in their use to signify simple acts of hate and defiance. We know true courage and bravery when we see them, and we will not lose sight of them.

16. Be unwavering and undeterred in proclaiming that the interests of American companies, workers, and citizens must be placed above all other interests when it comes to matters of policy.

17. Look directly at God, ourselves, and another human being every single day and say these words out loud: "I know who I am."

We, therefore, the free people of the United States of America, do solemnly publish and declare our new independence by declining to be codependent upon those who seek to do us harm. There can be no harsher sentence served upon a people than that of being held prisoner to the approval of others.

We recognize that in making this declination, we place ourselves at risk of various forms of reprisal. We do so, knowing that the truest expression, the fulfillment of individual freedom, is the willingness to place that freedom at risk for the purpose of preserving it, so that future generations of Americans might enjoy it.

As we join in this Declination, we do so with a firm reliance on the protection of divine Providence, and we mutually pledge to support each other with our lives, our fortunes, and our sacred honor.

INDEX

14th Amendment, 67
abortion, 42, 45, 51–53, 67–77, 90, 97, 115, 120, 128
Alinsky, Saul, 139, 140–141
Bentham, Jeremy, 191
Biden, Joe, 189, 191, 195, 197, 201
Blackstone, William, 19, 168, 210
Blazek, Felisa, iv, 3, 95, 155, 208
Bush, George W., 72
Charlottesville, Virginia, 47, 109, 126
Cicero, 19
Cloward, Richard, 138, 139
Common Ground Campus, 3, 95, 143, 155
Constitution, 14–15, 18–19, 28, 39, 52, 67, 71, 114, 162, 167, 198–200, 202, 210–211
Cronkite, Walter, 62, 67, 107
Declination of Codependence, 207, 210
Dissident, 155, 161, 163, 170, 172, 207
Enlightenment, 14, 162, 178, 191, 210
Fable of the Bees, 178
Ferguson, Missouri, 47, 77–78, 89, 110, 120, 126
Forgotten Man, 29–30
Frankfurt School, 136–137, 172
Franklin, Benjamin, 13–14, 70
French Revolution, 56–57
Freud, Sigmund, 136, 155, 194–195
Gugger, Jennifer, 158–159
Harari, Yuval Noah, 134, 194
Hitler, Adolph, 43, 45, 51–52, 58, 134, 136, 203
Hobbes, Thomas, 20–21, 26, 159, 162, 182, 192–196, 201
Hope College, 155, 173
House Un-American Activities Committee, 60–61
Hume, David, 48, 178, 191
Kant, Immanuel, 190–191
Kearney, Jane, 207
King, Martin Luther Jr., 138, 150

Kirk, Charlie, 1, 3, 161, 177
Labor Movement, 59, 70
Liberty Forum of Silicon Valley, 183, 207–208
Liberty Timeline, 27
Locke, John, 14, 19–21, 26, 84, 162, 168
Machiavelli, Niccolo, 139, 201
Madison, James, 14–15, 18–19
Mandeville, Bernard, 178
Marx, Karl, 23, 51, 136–137, 190
McCarthy, Joe, 60–62, 66
McVeigh, Timothy, 51–52
Menaker, Tatiana, 183–184
Mill, John Stuart, 191
Montesquieu, Charles, 19, 162, 168
Murrow, Edward, 61–62
Mussolini, Benito, 51–52, 58, 134
Navalny, Alexei, 158
neural pathing, 128–129, 132
New Deal, 28–29
opinion, 28, 65, 67–68, 83, 89–91, 99, 102, 106, 110–116, 119–120, 144, 192
Page, Wade Michael, 47–48, 52
Palecek, Peter, 183, 208
paraphrasing, 108–110, 118
Paul, Rand, 42–43, 45
perspective, 17, 21, 33, 88, 90, 99,–103, 106–108, 111, 120–121, 149, 174
Piven, Frances, 138–139
Popper, Karl, 18
prejudice, 100–108, 111, 118–119
Rand, Ayn, 51–52, 123, 182, 191
Reagan, Ronald, 142–143, 183
Roe v. Wade, 67
Santorum, Rick, 51–52
Smith, Adam, 162, 178, 191, 193–196
Solzhenitsyn, Alexander, 182, 187
South Dakota, 207, 209
Springsteen, Bruce, 35–36
Stalin, Joseph, 58, 203
state of nature, 20–21, 84, 192

Sumner, William, 29–30
Team Right-Team Left, 2, 46, 66
Trump, Donald, 16, 73, 97, 107–110, 120,
    124, 126–127, 160, 162, 180, 189,
    191, 196–197, 201
Turner Diaries, 48, 52
Vietnam War, 64–66, 81, 107, 127
Wałęsa, Lech, 175, 182
Wolf, Naomi, 79, 80, 183

www.ingramcontent.com/pod-product-compliance
Lightning Source LLC
Chambersburg PA
CBHW071955260326
41914CB00004B/804